The Pope Who Quit

The Pope Who Quit

A TRUE MEDIEVAL TALE OF MYSTERY, DEATH, AND SALVATION

JON M. SWEENEY

Image Books

New York

IMAGE

IMAGE and the Image colophon are registered trademarks of Random
House, Inc.

ISBN 978-1-61793-877-1

PRINTED IN THE UNITED STATES OF AMERICA

Cover design by Rebecca Lown
Cover art: © Réunion des Musées Nationaux/Art Resource, NY

Book Club Edition

In memory of

Violet "San Romani" Grundman

1916–2010

CONTENTS

viii   CONTENTS

TIME LINE OF KEY EVENTS

CA. 1209–10 Peter Angelerio is born in a small village in Molise, the most remote region of Italy.

1230 After spending three years as a monk at Santa Maria of Faifula, Peter leaves to become a hermit in the mountains.

1231–44 He founds a new religious order on and around Mount Morrone, in the Abruzzo region of southern Italy; this order will become known as the Celestine Hermits half a century later.

CA. 1240–CA. 1290 Little is known about Peter's daily doings for these nearly fifty years.

1281 Benedict Gaetani is made a cardinal by Pope Martin IV.

APRIL 1292 Pope Nicholas IV dies in Rome. Twelve cardinals assemble to elect the next pope. They remain stalemated for twenty-seven months.

MARCH 1294 Charles II, king of Naples, offers a list of names to the cardinals. These are rejected.

JUNE 1294   The cardinals reassemble in Perugia. Peter writes a letter of apocalyptic foreboding to Latino Malabranca Orsini, dean of the Sacred College.

JULY 5, 1294   Malabranca receives Peter's letter and is inspired to offer up the hermit's name as the next supreme pontiff.

AUGUST 29, 1294   Peter takes the angelic name Celestine V and is crowned in the basilica of Santa Maria of Collemaggio in L'Aquila.[1] He remains within the Kingdom of Naples throughout his papacy at the urging of Charles II.

NOVEMBER 1294   Celestine creates a wooden hut in the papal apartments in Castle Nuovo, preferring to live humbly in the midst of splendor. He attempts, but fails, to put a triad of cardinals in charge of most papal duties.

DECEMBER 13, 1294   Celestine abdicates with Cardinal Gaetani's help.

CHRISTMAS EVE 1294   Gaetani is elected Pope Boniface VIII.

CHRISTMASTIDE 1294   Boniface VIII orders Peter Celestine found and imprisoned.

MAY 19, 1296   Peter dies in Castle Fumone, near Anagni.

CA. 1310–12   In his elaborate allegory of the afterlife, Dante places Peter, not in Hell itself, but just outside its gates.

MARCH 5, 1313   Clement V canonizes Saint Celestine V from the new papal home in Avignon, France.

The Pope Who Quit

No man save One, since Adam, has been wholly good.
Not one has been wholly bad.
—FREDERICK ROLFE

PROLOGUE

Toward the close of the Middle Ages, in 1285, there lived three men whose lives would intersect and forever change history. Each was a man of power. Each was stubborn. Each was skilled at the life and work to which he seemed destined from birth.

The most important of the three and the central figure of this book is Peter Morrone. His surname comes from the mountain that he called home for most of his life. Peter was a monk and the founder of a religious order, and depending on whom you talk to, he was also a reformer, an instigator, a prophet, a coward, a fool, and a saint. He was very much a man swept up in history, and practically overnight he would be transformed from a humble hermit into Pope Celestine V, the most powerful man in the Catholic Church. He would also become the only man in history to walk away from his job, vacating the chair of St. Peter before he died.

If Peter Morrone lived today in the mountains outside of Rome or Los Angeles or New Delhi he might be a celebrity guru. From early in his life he was a man with a mountain, or *montagna,* and made his *casa di montagna.* If he'd lived in the twenty-first century, talks to his fellow monks might be smuggled out of his enclave as digital audio files, soon to be packaged and sold by a big New York concern. He would emerge every now and then to speak privately with world leaders, who would also seek him out for personal counsel and, perhaps, photo opportunities. Peter was this sort of figure in his day.

But history rarely revolves around a single individual, and the story of Peter Morrone-cum-Celestine V is no exception. Although fellow monks and supporters would move in and out of Peter's rather long life, there are two men in particular whose power and ambition would directly affect the life of this complex hermit, and, by extension, their actions would influence the world.

The first of these was Charles II of Anjou (1254–1309), supporter, corruptor, the ingratiating king of Naples. Having inherited his crown from a much more powerful father in January 1285, Charles II learned quickly how to use influential men, as well as to be of use to them. Charles would keep the hermit pope on a tight leash.

The second man who is central to our story is Cardinal Benedict Gaetani, one of the eleven cardinal-electors who chose Peter Morrone as pope. Born as Benedetto, son of Gaetani, into a prominent family in about 1235, he was a true Roman and the nephew of Pope Alexander IV (1254–61). Well educated from youth, he trained as a lawyer, was skilled in canon law, and was made a member of the curia at the age of twenty-nine. For the next thirty years Gaetani gained a reputation as a supremely competent papal legate who could represent the Holy See in confronting heresy and spiritual rebellion in places like

England and France, asserting moral authority when heretical movements rose to the surface. He would become Celestine V's trusted adviser and would help the hermit pope resign from office—perhaps conniving for his own self-interest because he would take the chair of St. Peter only eleven days later.

Celestine V's abdication was the climax of a five-month reign, from July to December of 1294, during which time he served as Christ's supreme representative on earth, and then quit. As we will see, nothing went well for anyone, except perhaps for Gaetani.

When a man is raised to the chair of St. Peter he is not elected for a certain term or period of time. He becomes pope for life. Yet throughout the 2,000-year history of the papacy Peter Morrone is the only man who has resigned and walked away.

There are three reasons I wanted to tell this story. First, I have a fascination with the Middle Ages. In particular, the twelfth and thirteenth centuries were a time of faith, violence, and discovery, a time that is replete with dramatic stories and pivotal moments. I have written and edited a number of books on the lives and impact of some of this period's most colorful and recognizable figures, such as Francis of Assisi. In contrast, the colorful story of Celestine V is hardly known.[1]

I first heard about Celestine V a decade ago while doing research in Italy for a book about the inheritors of the spiritual legacy of Saint Francis. This "angelic pope"—as some of his contemporaries called him—was condemned to mill around outside the gates of the *Inferno* for eternity by Dante, who may have actually known him. Dante wrote, "I looked, and I beheld the shade of him / Who made through cowardice the great refusal."[2] This was the poet's way of saying that our subject was a quitter and a weakling. But how could Celestine be both "angelic" and "cowardly"? How could he be pope and also deserving of hell? Clearly, there's a bundle of contradictions to this story that need to be sorted out.

Further, I wondered how history would be different if Celestine had stayed in power, or if he'd met with any success whatsoever as holy father during the fifteen weeks of his reign. How did his election fill the imaginations of everyday people with hope for change? How did his disastrous reign bring that hope to an end? "Was he conquered by his innate powerlessness, or by a combination of abnormal rascality and intrigue?" asked the English writer Anne MacDonell a century ago.[3] These questions I set out to answer.

As a cradle Protestant who converted to Catholicism after a number of years of searching and discernment, I'm probably drawn more quickly than others to stories of spiritual reformers. Celestine in his heart was a reformer. During the sixty years he spent as a hermit, he responded to laxity with stern measures, and sought a return to original principles. He could not find a religious order that would allow him to pray and fast, nor could he find the solitude he required. In founding his own ascetical order he modeled it on the legends of John the Baptist, living deliberately in desert-like conditions of want, wearing a hair shirt as penance, and fasting continuously (except on Sunday). Peter's desires for a Church that did what was right were legendary. Some over the years have seen him as a forerunner of later Catholics such as Martin Luther, whose writings set off the Protestant Reformation, resulting in a complete split of the world's religious strata. But that comparison is far-fetched. Nothing of that sort would have ever occurred to Peter Morrone, let alone to the reform-minded in 1294. Still one explanation for the perplexities of his life was that he was an idealist.

Third, Peter Morrone aka Celestine V (you'll notice that I use both names throughout the book) is still making headlines in the twenty-first century. A year after I began my research, on April 6, 2009, an earthquake hit L'Aquila, Italy, shaking everything, including the walls of the great church that Peter Morrone built and in which he was later buried. Aftershocks followed for the next two days, and one of those brought the ornate roof of the basilica crashing down into the nave. On April 8, 2009, media all over the world reported on firefighters rushing into the building to retrieve the sacred remains and relics of this angelic pope. The essentials of Celestine V's story were told and retold for days. The saint's remains were placed in safer quarters and then brought back to the basilica in a glass casket. In contemporary times prominent Catholics differ quite considerably from Dante in their assessment of Celestine. They were quoted in Italian newspapers referring to the discovery of the unharmed remains as yet another miracle at the hand of Saint Celestine V (he was canonized seventeen years after his death, and miracles of all sorts have been attributed to his intercession over the last six hundred years).

Four years earlier, in the winter of 2004–5, Celestine was also discussed in media throughout the world when the Vatican's secretary of state hinted that the ailing Pope John Paul II was considering retirement. Celestine was featured in print and cinema as a result of Dan Brown's blockbuster *Angels & Demons* (chapter 88 of the book, published in 2000; and then in the film, 2009). Yet Brown wasn't the first modern writer to mention Celestine.

The angelic pope was the subject of a historical novel by Ignazio Silone, published in Italian in 1968 and in English as *The Story of a Humble Christian* in 1970. The London playwright Peter Barnes wrote about Celestine in *Sunsets and Glories*, which premiered in Leeds, England, in June 1990. And I suspect that the story of Peter must have inspired Morris West to write his blockbuster novel *The Clowns of God* (1981) about a fictional twentieth-century pope who abdicates under duress. *The Clowns of God* spent twenty-two weeks on the *New York Times* bestseller list when it was released in hardcover.

And then there is one final reason that the topic of this book should interest readers today—and this emerged after I began writing. Pope Benedict XVI has recently aligned himself with the memory and legacy of this hermit pope from the medieval Catholic past. On April 29, 2009, when Pope Benedict visited Celestine's tomb in the aftermath of the earthquake that struck L'Aquila earlier in the month he did more than say a simple prayer and pay his respects at the Italian saint's shrine. Without explanation the pope paused for several minutes, removed the pallium from around his shoulders, and laid it gently on Celestine's glass-encased tomb. A pallium is a religious garment that is shaped like a Y and resembles a long, stiff scarf. It is one of the principal symbols of a pope's episcopal authority. It seems that Pope Benedict was communicating that something lies unfinished in the worldwide Catholic Church, and it is somehow connected with Celestine V.

There are very few firsthand accounts of the life of the famous man who left the Chair of St. Peter empty. The Middle Ages is a time for which we have no attendance records at schools, no physician's records or census records. The most reliable sources of information are court and church annals, but those records that have not been lost to fire or the elements can be unreliable. There is often almost nothing to firmly place a person on the planet in those days. Illiteracy was common, and few people wrote about themselves and others. In fact, one of the reasons that Celestine V's election as pope was so controversial was that he was seen as unschooled compared to the privileged men who held important ecclesiastical offices. And he understood very little Latin, the official language of the Church.

In telling Peter's story I have relied on a variety of sources. Peter wrote an Autobiography, which was unusual for that era, and we can trust it for some of the details of his early life. In addition, I have combed through histories of the medieval papacy, in which Celestine V stands out but only as one curiosity among many. There are many histories of the mendicant orders (all five, including the Franciscans and Dominicans, were founded in Peter's lifetime), medieval hermits, heretical movements, and the multifaceted Crusades (the fifth through ninth occurred while Peter was living), from which I gleaned many of the details herein. We are witnessing rapid growth in the availability of English translations of documents from this time period in Italy; these works illuminate subjects such as the local structures of religious and secular power, the dependence of rural areas on the cities, warfare and violence, law and order, disease and medicine, education, and family.[4] I have used these sources and more to paint a picture of Peter's era, his places, his people, and the circumstances of his life.

There are additional historical records of thirteenth-century Catholic piety, local religious rituals, infighting between factions within the Church, the growing independence of laypeople—all of which serve to illuminate Peter's actions as a sibling, son, hermit, abbot, founder of an order, traveling pilgrim, builder of churches, sinner, penitent, fund-raiser, and faithful Catholic. I describe Peter and characters in Peter's story, and I imagine his spiritual brothers who sat with him at the end of his life in a castle prison cell and listened as he told them stories. I cast a spotlight on the members of the papal curia (advisers, administrators, counselors, financial managers) who surrounded and confounded Celestine during his fifteen disastrous weeks as Christ's vicar. Some of these scenes are imagined after spending many hours looking at manuscript illuminations, scrutinizing paintings (there are just a few renderings of him), and reading letters and historical accounts of men and women from the place and time. Using all of these resources, I aim to tell the story of what it was like to be a hermit and a pope in the turbulent, hopeful, and violent late thirteenth century.

INTRODUCTION

A World Gone Crazy

No one knew precisely where the march had begun, but it was rumored to have its origins in Perugia, that ancient Etruscan city proudly sitting a thousand feet above the Tiber River, and it appeared to be slowly making its way south toward Rome. A simple man named Raneiro led this group on a Sunday afternoon. If he didn't look so dour and serious, the unsuspecting villagers might have mistaken their predawn visitors for one of the wandering theatrical troupes that frequented these parts of Italy. But this was no troupe; the people weren't hungover or sleepy or even remotely jocular, and they weren't wandering. Raneiro's march was a planned procession of converts.

Spectators watched as this ragtag group of ordinary working Italians walked mostly single file and barefoot, the one in front carrying a banner bearing an illustration, rough woven in wool and satin, of the scourging of Christ. On that emblem the Lord God was depicted standing with his hands tied behind his back, nothing but a rag wrapped around his slender waist, while two burly soldiers whipped him. The barefoot converts sang songs and chants, mostly to the Virgin Mary. Their procession had been winding its way from village to village throughout Umbria, on either side of the Tiber River, picking up new members along the way. They called themselves the *disciplinati*.

Self-flagellation has been around since the Middle Ages, but Dan Brown sensationalized the practice by including in *The Da Vinci Code* an evil albino monk who whips himself in private each evening as a spiritual practice. Yes, people still do it. The custom is one among a collection of practices called Christian mortification. A Roman Catholic order of nearly 100,000 people called Opus Dei quietly advocates "the discipline" as a way of taming the body's appetites and participating in the sufferings of Christ. In fact, in early 2010 Slawomir Oder, the Polish monsignor overseeing the cause in Rome for John Paul II, disclosed in a new book that John Paul II was a self-flagellator. He even took his whip with him on vacation.[1]

Once they had gathered in the village center, the disciplinati began to unpack satchels containing their instruments of self-torture. Raneiro slung his bag from his shoulder and plunked it on the cobblestones. He was rail thin, but his wool hair shirt added a little bulk to his emaciated frame. Hair shirts at the time were almost a layperson's monastic "habit." For many, a monk's generous habit had come to stand for a life of easy excess, and not asceticism. Oftentimes only the highborn or most naturally gifted were admitted to the best monasteries, and those monasteries were often the only places in a region where sumptuous food, plenty of drink, and personal safety were to be had. The man beneath the habit was often the most portly man around. In contrast, the wearing of a hair shirt represented a truer commitment.

The disciplinati were inspired by the new religious orders that were springing up during Peter Morrone's lifetime, among them the Franciscans and Dominicans, who dedicated their lives to chastity and poverty. Ordinary folk sometimes wore chains around the torso or in other private places hidden beneath clothing, making daily movement deliberately difficult and uncomfortable. Other practices, such as giving up the commonly accepted comforts of extra clothing or soft beds, became common as well. These lay penitents were known to sleep on wooden boards and go without shoes even in the harshness of winter. The practice of being "discalced," or without shoes, has roots in the Desert Fathers and Mothers of late antiquity, and was intermittently practiced by thousands of penitents in the thirteenth century.

These Christians practiced their asceticism in the streets. Some of them lived simply, worked, and raised their families around Rome. Some were full-time pilgrims on their way to Rome to see the places where Saint Paul and Saint Peter were martyred for the faith, or to Compostela in Spain to view the relics of the apostle James. Their focus was on personal penitence, but they also advocated public and corporate displays of repentance for sins: they were witnessing to the need to repent for the faults of the Church at large, just as Christ had once assumed the sins of the world, hanging them upon a cross. The spread of these practices often coincided with a flaring up of the plague that was ravishing cities and villages throughout Europe. Ordinary citizens often believed that infectious disease was a form of divine judgment on them, so they began to do penance to satisfy God. Lay preachers would stand in the public squares during rallies and preach for days to all who would listen. The actions of flagellants and other groups of penitents often took the form of what we'd recognize today as protests, and seemed to be aimed at communicating warnings to their ecclesiastical leadership. They would chant things such as "We beat ourselves so that God does not have to."[2] As they tried to assume personal and spiritual responsibility for troubles that were bigger than themselves, they also carried around a feeling of dread. What did the future hold? Was the end of the world at hand?

Most of the disciplinati men were already bare to the waist. It was eighty degrees in the early morning air, with the sun beating down. Raneiro removed his rough cord whip, with thorns embedded in the knots at the ends, designed to lacerate the skin, and he untangled the strands. Then he began to strike himself. *Flagellum* means "whip" in Latin. Grabbing the handle of the whip in his right hand, he snapped it over his left shoulder again and again, slowly and methodically, holding his left hand firm against his abdomen.

What were Raneiro's motives? Why was he doing this to himself? Just as the people of Nineveh avoided destruction at the hands of an angry God by fasting and putting on sackcloth (according to the book of Jonah), the flagellants making their way toward Rome were demonstrating to God that they wanted to repent for whatever humankind had done to bring on the plague, war, corruption, storms, and violence that they were experiencing.

Not long ago flagellants and other "religious enthusiasts" were written off as simply "hot-blooded." Victorian-era scholars wrote books for armchair enthusiasts about people from other cultures and eras who demonstrated passion for religious faith that seemed, to them at least, foreign. But that was the Victorian era; from the vantage point of the twenty-first century we can see how religion and passion intimately and easily intermingle. Nevertheless, the enthusiasm of thirteenth-century flagellants was not typical of most Catholics. This generation had watched the rise of Gothic cathedrals. This was the time when Thomas Aquinas and Albertus Magnus were teaching students at the University of Paris, and universities were still a new idea. So while Chartres was rising like a skyscraper and Aquinas was writing a hundred volumes of theological commentary on every subject imaginable, why is it that outside the courtyards of bishops' residences and village cathedrals it seemed that the world was going mad? Right in the middle of the city square, some Christians were reduced to whipping themselves raw.

Children flocked into the city center like swallows at the first sounds of the approaching group. Mocking, at first, they then stood enraptured, waiting for the show, only to laugh with a certain horror and then scatter before the pigeons began to lap up the blood.

The disciplinati were the conservatives of their day. These particular ones were antigovernment, weary of corrupt local lords as well as King Manfred and his German knights, whose rule was about to end in the Kingdom of Naples and Sicily. They desired more local control over their lives and they expected greater moral fortitude in their leaders. They were a missionary movement, creating their own holy crusade through self-inflicted torture and confession to show religious leaders that conversion begins right here and right now—on the flesh and shoulders of the penitent—rather than in some far-off land. And they were among the first people of the Middle Ages to become spiritually self-determining: they were finished with being told what was just and holy by ecclesiastical leaders who were usually anything but.

A Hermit's Life

Peter Morrone knew many among this order of flagellants. He watched them with interest. He shared some of their ideas. But he was not one of them. He was a quiet man, he was poor, and he was a hermit.

Peter walked barefoot in the name of God among the cities of the Abruzzi, the Marches, and Umbria, traversing Italian villages and mountain retreats and bishoprics with his brothers in order to secure income and protection for their churches and hermitages. He was in many respects a common beggar, but a beggar in the name of Christ.

When we imagine a hermit some of us think of a crazy, misanthropic sort of character. Neither characterization is true of Peter. We might also imagine a recluse with long fingernails and matted dirty hair. Peter may have fit this description. But in essentials he was a man who had separated himself from the world. He lived austerely, as a visible reminder to other Christians—bishops, priests, cloistered monks—that Jesus went to the desert to fast and be tempted by the devil. The Gospels tell of Jesus going off to be alone on several occasions, including in the final decisive moments in the Garden of Gethsemane before the soldiers arrested him. Hermits did not live in homes. They didn't aspire to anything permanent. They lived as self-consciously as the one who said of himself, "Foxes have holes, and birds of the air have nests; but the Son of Man has nowhere to lay his head."[3]

Hermits inhabited caves and huts, sometimes lean-tos that were attached to larger buildings, and they lived always in a way that de-emphasized the values that others around them placed on a settled domestic life of marriage, children, and possessions. Jesus called his disciples out of the world, telling them to follow him totally and completely. Hermits took these words literally. "Look at the birds of the air: they neither sow nor reap nor gather into barns, and yet your heavenly Father feeds them," Jesus said (Mt. 6:26). So, like the birds, a hermit was supposed to live without planning for the future. He had foresworn the comforts of a wife or children. He called his home a tomb, for he had already "died" to the world.

We have no descriptions of Peter's appearance, and the only paintings of him that still exist depict him when he was in his eighties. But as a robust adult he was surely thickly bearded, with dark hair in clotted locks, for it would have been rarely washed or combed. We know that he was several inches taller than the average man of his day, his height emphasized by his uncommonly erect stature. In those days height was usually taken to be a sign of upright integrity. The medieval mind was captivated by physiological determinism: the notion that a person's physical traits are indications of his character. To have a high nose was to be haughty. To have a large head was to be intelligent. That is why we see in old stories the eye patch of a pirate symbolizing his craftiness. The curvature of a moneylender's spine indicates his conniving. The long, unbound hair of a woman shows that she is of loose morals. And so it goes. A hunchback doesn't grow up to be an archbishop or pope.

Rail thin from a lifetime of ascetic practice, Peter wasn't lithe but he was vigorous. He had the stature and bearing of a man with power. Medieval men often chose between power that was *regnum* (royal) and power that was *sacerdo-tium* (priestly), but Peter was destined to live both. Even in his eighties, when he was elected pope, Peter was a *presence*.

After his death, the people of Sulmona, the city closest to Mount Morrone, would testify that his asceticism was so severe as to make his body appear tormented. He was grizzled and worn. Peter lived a difficult sort of a life. He dressed in the religious garb he'd chosen for his monks, namely, a grey habit (emphasizing lowliness) and a starkly contrasting dark hood (signifying death). He looked the part of the penitent. "Only divine grace could allow him to remain alive," those who knew him said, and just looking at his tortured face moved many people to tears.[4]

Hermits were only one of many spiritual types that kindled the imaginations of people who lived more or-dinary lives in villages and towns. These were the days of traveling mystics, new religious movements, warrior monks, street ascetics, and spiritual wonders. Among them Knights Templar and Teutonic Knights were the most val-iant and colorful figures of the day; they were the heroes of the Crusades. The first recorded case of someone re-ceiving the stigmata also occurred in Peter's lifetime—it happened to Saint Francis of Assisi, in Umbria in 1224. Many Christians, whose lives consisted of little more than a series of boring, repetitive, everyday acts, made claims to extraordinary mystical experiences. Figures and events such as these filled the minds of the women and men of Peter's century.

But corruption and violence were very much on people's minds as well. Kings, knights, and mercenaries routinely invaded the lands of Italy throughout the cen-tury, competing to govern more territory and to make themselves richer by levying taxes on the citizens who remained. Local civic leaders attempted to keep order. Religious leaders tried, usually in vain, to negotiate for peace. But more often than not, ordinary people either sought refuge from corruption, violence, disease, and other common hardships by entering religious life (if they were fortunate enough to be accepted by one of the monasteries or convents), or they kept their heads down and tried to work out their lives as best they could while hoping for something better.

Occasionally, a holy man would emerge who could break through the old patterns and ways of being. People believed in those portions of the Bible that spoke of prophets, leaders, liberators, and the Messiah. After Abraham came Moses; after Moses, David; from David, Jesus. Jesus, they knew, would return someday, and preparing the way for him would be good men such as Saint Francis of Assisi, whom some still remembered. The prophet Isaiah once foretold:

> *A voice cries:*
> *"In the wilderness prepare the way of the Lord,*
> *make straight in the desert a highway for our God.*
> *Every valley shall be lifted up,*
> *and every mountain and hill be made low;*
> *the uneven ground shall become level,*
> *and the rough places a plain.*
> *And the glory of the Lord shall be revealed,*
> *and all flesh shall see it together,*
> *for the mouth of the Lord has spoken."* (Is. 40:3–5)

Despite their troubles, people still believed that a truly honest and good man might one day be found who might save Christ's church, the world, and their souls.

PART I
WHEN THE UNEXPECTED HAPPENED

Peter Morrone . . . my heart was filled with anxious grief

When you pronounced the words, "I will!"

For that yoke might lay upon your neck

Only to damn your soul to Hell.

—JACOPONE OF TODI,
"Epistle to Pope Celestine V"

A LETTER THAT CHANGED
JUST ABOUT EVERYTHING

Despite the power of his physical presence—or perhaps, *because of it*—Peter Morrone preferred writing to oratory. This is not surprising. The man, after all, was a hermit, and although the word didn't exist back then, it's safe to say that the monk with the body of an athlete and the heart of a rebel was an *introvert*. When he had something to say, more often than not, he wrote a letter.

The word *hermit* comes from Latin and Greek and literally means "of the desert." For millennia a hermit has been a man who aims to live mostly alone in order to pray and work out his salvation. The prophet Elijah was a Hebrew hermit who lived centuries before Christ. John the Baptist was living as a hermit in the Land of Israel along the Jordan River before Jesus began his adult ministry. In the fourth century Christian hermits sometimes went to "the desert"—any lonely or remote place—in order to learn to more fully and completely love others. They needed very little, but in their poverty they believed they could most directly understand Christ.

On one particular occasion an eighty-four-year-old hermit was desperate to make his feelings known. The College of Cardinals was taking far too long to select the next pope, and something had to be done.

Peter believed that the cardinals should consider the implications of their seemingly endless deliberations. *We won't have another interregnum!* he probably said to a brother monk, standing outside the entrance to his cave. Broadly speaking, an "interregnum" is the time that lapses between the death of one pope and the election of a new one. But by 1294 the term had come to stand for a notorious vacancy of the papacy that was still fresh in people's minds—the three years between 1268 and 1271.

After Clement IV died in 1268, for two years the cardinal-electors were bickering and fighting, meeting and adjourning in the Palazzo dei Papi, or "Palace of the Popes," in Viterbo, refusing to lay down their self-interests in order to elect a successor to the chair of St. Peter. So the people of Viterbo locked the sixteen cardinals inside, laid siege to the palace, bricking up the entrances, allowing only bread and water to be passed through, insisting that the cardinal-electors finally choose a man for the job. The siege lasted for more than twelve months. Still nothing. Then, when the patience of the people had reached its limit, piece by piece the people removed the roof above the room in which the cardinals were meeting, letting in hot sunshine and pouring rain. Within three days Tebaldo Visconti was elected Pope Gregory X by a compromise delegation of six cardinals. And when it was all over and the cardinals emerged looking well fed, as usual, the people realized that the cardinal-electors must have had secret access to other food and supplies. Four of those sixteen cardinal-electors went on to become mostly unimpressive popes themselves: Adrian V (r. July 11–August 18, 1276), Nicholas III (r. 1277–80), Martin IV (r. 1281–85), and Honorius IV (r. 1285–87).

In the summer of 1294, Peter looked down into the valley below him. The land was lush with verdant greens, but he knew that not far from where he stood the cardinals of Mother Church were once again divided, avoiding their duty, refusing to come to a consensus about the future.

Like a Desert Father in Syria or Upper Egypt in the fourth century, living just enough on the outskirts of the cities to be out of reach of Roman authority, Peter lived in what was considered the most remote region of Italy: the mountains of Abruzzi, seventy miles east of Rome. From his perch he was as much the inheritor of the poet Horace's powerful ideal of *rusticorum mascula* ("masculine offspring") as he was one of Jesus' followers seeking to be meek in order to inherit the earth.[1] In lifestyle, he was closer to John the Baptist than he was to the cardinals, or "princes," of the Church.

From the mountains Peter was in a good position to see clearly what the Church needed most. His was an ancient perspective: that rough living and landscape built moral character and men of the mountains could see what those in cities could not.[2] Although Peter would not have presumed to consider himself a prophet, his actions parallel those of the Hebrew prophets who were always outsiders pointing out what was going wrong. Peter's message in his letter to Cardinal Malabranca is, in fact, reminiscent of something Isaiah said:

> *The Spirit of the Lord God is upon me,*
> *because the Lord has anointed me*

to bring good news to the afflicted;
  he has sent me to bind up the brokenhearted,
to proclaim liberty to the captives,
  and the opening of the prison to those who are bound.

Or Saint John the Divine who said: "I was in the spirit on the Lord's day, and I heard behind me a loud voice like a trumpet saying, 'Write what you see in a book and send it to the seven churches, to Ephesus and to Smyrna and to Pergamum and to Thyatira and to Sardis and to Philadelphia and to Laodicea'" (Is. 61:1; and Rv. 1:10–11).

By the summer of 1294, Peter was revered for his age and wisdom. At eighty-four, he was an old man, but Saint Anthony of Egypt lived to be 105, Peter would have reminded his monks. And Saint Paul of Thebes, Anthony's teacher, lived even longer. Saint Jerome, too, was often visited by angels during the decades of old age that he spent living alone near Bethlehem. Every hermit knew such things.

There have been a few occasions when a letter has changed the course of history.[3] This was one of those times. The letter Peter wrote was both private and intended to provoke. Because of his religious celebrity reputation, any communication from Peter would be unusual, even for the College of Cardinals meeting in Perugia.

The letter would have looked rather ordinary. Various types of wood were common for letter-writing during this period, and bark was the most portable of them all. It might seem that bark would be too perishable to be used for a letter written to a cardinal, but in the hands of a hermit that humble material might have had just the effect that was intended. Paper, as opposed to the animal skins used for parchment, was even more impermanent in those days since it was made from rags and "other more vile material," as Peter the Venerable once put it.[4]

The actual letter is no longer extant. Perhaps a cardinal accidentally threw it into the fire with a previous round's ballots, or maybe it was tucked into the pages of a Latin codex, and is still extant, 750 years later, lost in a library somewhere in Europe. All we know is that the letter was written in June 1294 and was addressed to Cardinal Latino Malabranca Orsini, dean of the College of Cardinals. The letter was written in Latin, which means that if Peter wrote it himself the writing would have been unskilled because, as sources tell us, he was largely uneducated. And we can surmise that the missive was delivered by a younger monk who could maneuver down the rocks and inclines better than a vibrant octogenarian.

I can imagine Peter instructing the young monk charged with delivering his letter to the Sacred College.

Brother, pronto! Presto!

The letter delivered in person to Malabranca on the morning of July 5, 1294, was, according to the venerable hagiographer Alban Butler, filled with "holy rage." What did the letter say?

> God's judgment falls on those who ignore His will, and on those who are willingly blind in seeking it. You and the others have been like ones charged with restoring a roof to a beautiful house, and yet you leave the tools and plans at home for years on end, leaving those inside to burn in the hot sun and freeze to death during blazing summers and dread winters. The inaction you have shown will

surely bring the wrath of Jesus Christ down upon you, upon your families, and upon all of us who call ourselves by his name.

We can't be certain that these were Peter's exact words, but these were the ideas and feelings communicated—and something in that letter inspired the cardinal, because we know for certain that he quickly nominated Peter as the next ruler of God's Church on earth.

THE BIZARRE PAPAL ELECTION
OF 1292–94

Two years earlier, on April 4, 1292, Pope Nicholas IV, a man whom many had called "the good Franciscan," because he was the first of Francis of Assisi's spiritual progeny to rise to the papacy, lay dead in Rome, leaving the chair of St. Peter vacant.

Nicholas was born Girolamo Masci and raised in the Marche region of central Italy, approximately 120 miles (circumnavigating the Apennine Mountains from the Marches north to the Adriatic, then south from there to the Abruzzi) from Peter's home in the Abruzzi. These remote places of Italy often give one the impression that there are more mountain pines than people. Before becoming pope, Girolamo had been elected minister-general of the Franciscans to replace Saint Bonaventure, the influential friar who'd rewritten the Life of Francis and ordered destroyed all earlier versions written by men who knew the saint best. This was a century when the lines between sanctity, power, and violence can be difficult to discern, and, curiously, the diary of Bonaventure's secretary was discovered and published only a century ago. In it we learn that the theologian fell victim to a fate not uncommon in those days: murder. He was poisoned, to be exact, most likely by one of his own spiritual brethren.

After Girolamo succeeded Bonaventure, three years later he was made Latin Patriarch of Constantinople, a position created by the Crusades. He lived in conquered Constantinople, governing the Western Church precariously beside the Eastern Church's Patriarch for three years. In 1281, he moved back to Italy to serve as the cardinal-bishop in Palestrina, and from that position he was elected pope in 1287.

By most accounts, Nicholas IV's record as pontiff was solid. He was reluctant to accept the post, and in fact was elected by his colleagues in the College twice, in rapid succession, in order to demonstrate how sincerely they believed he was the man for the job. Nicholas IV combined the spiritual sensitivity of a good follower of Saint Francis with the acumen of a world ruler, skills he had learned abroad.

The thirteenth century was a time of creative intensity, not just in Italy, but around the world. It was an era of invention, intellectual curiosity, and adventure. For example, it was in the mid-thirteenth century that gunpowder was first used in a cannon in a land battle between the Mamluks and the Mongols in the Jezreel Valley of Palestine. The use of gunpowder is one of the primary reasons that the Mamluks were able to deliver the Mongols their first, real military defeat, keeping them from advancing toward Egypt. Later in the century, land mines were first used by Song Dynasty Chinese against Mongol invaders in southern China. Meanwhile, across Europe there was an awakened interest in the principles of Hippocrates, leading to the first accurate descriptions of diseases, medical conditions, and cures. Theories explaining the process of circulation of the blood as well as developments in surgery—most of which originated in the East with thinkers such as Averroes (d. 1198) and Ibn al-Nafis (d. 1288)—advanced modern medicine. Public intellectuals emerged in this century as well, through the burgeoning of universities. Men such as the Franciscan philosopher Roger Bacon (ca. 1214–94), his era's *Doctor Mirabilis,* or "Wonderful Teacher," began to focus on empirical methods of reasoning. Combined with the advancement of knowledge from philosophers in the Muslim East, this led to a gradual collapse of the authority approach to knowledge. Hypothesis, research, and evidence came increasingly into play. No longer were the ideas of a previous era's experts automatically the starting point for the future. Just as Copernicus would soon reject the ideas of Ptolemy in the study of astronomy, so too did physicians and philosophers of the late thirteenth century begin to dispense with the best wisdom of the early Middle Ages in favor of new researches.

Other social changes were under way, as well. Laborers began forming workers' guilds and planting the seeds that would give rise to the middle class in the centuries to follow. Powerful mayors and towns began to form as local economies strengthened because of enhanced transportation and trade, leading to the breakdown of old models of serfdom. People became more mobile than ever before, traveling outside their local parishes and provinces, on roads rediscovered and refurbished from the golden travel age of the Roman Empire. People's lives were no longer completely determined by the situation into which they had been born. And religious life was undergoing rapid change and evolution, fueled by the energy of lay reform movements as well as the new Franciscan and Dominican orders. Early versions of boardinghouses and hostels were popping up to accommodate the pilgrims, friars, and wandering ascetics all about. All of this led to a vibrancy of intellectual, civic, and religious life never before seen.

In other respects, Western Europe and Mother Church were in dire straits. Both were in need of a savior. The center of the world was identified on maps that depicted Asia to Africa to Europe seen from a "birds-eye," godlike perspective. At the center of the earth was the city of Jerusalem, and beside Jerusalem the hidden location of the lost Garden of Eden. The Holy Land was the pivot upon which the world turned. But it was still in Muslim hands.

Christian fervor to get it back had led to the first of the Crusades in 1095. Over the next two hundred years Christianity warred against Islam (and sometimes Eastern Christians, and usually Jews), and in the process families and inheritances were decimated (the orderly transfer of power from father to son was broken because so many sons were dead). It has been estimated that the capital lost during this time was staggering. To take one small example, the saintly King Louis IX of France is said to have spent six times the annual income of his throne (arming and provisioning 15,000 men and at least thirty-six ships) in order to recover a few relics of Christ's Passion from the Holy Land to fill Sainte-Chapelle, the chapel he was building back in Paris.[1]

When he'd first ascended to the papacy in February 1288, Nicholas IV had offered new hope of success with regard to taking back Jerusalem, but it wasn't to be. Tales of crusading victories as well as devastating defeat had been traveling home to Italy for nearly two centuries, and then the whole movement was dealt a death blow in the spring of 1291. The flow of princes, militant monks, and their recruits seeking adventure, riches, and eternal life came to an abrupt end when Acre, the fortress stronghold on Haifa Bay, capital of the Christian Kingdom of Jerusalem since 1192, fell to well-organized Muslim troops after a siege. Acre is in what is today northern Israel and was the site of all Western Christianity's communication and travel in and out of the Holy Land. The fortress was inhabited by crusaders of all kinds, including Templars, Hospitallers, and knights from all over Europe with varying motivations, some good and some not so good. An estimated 40,000 Christians were living in Acre when the outpost fell on May 18, 1291. Within months, all the other nearby Christian footholds in the Holy Land had fallen too. These events took place at the tail end of Nicholas's pontificate. To retain a foothold in the land where the Savior had walked meant everything to serious Christians of that era, and many believed that the calamity at Acre had occurred because of a lack of strength in the papacy.[2] To illustrate, the playwright Peter Barnes offers this opening scene in his play about the life of Pope Celestine V: The most prominent cardinals of the Sacred College are standing in a Vatican antechamber bickering over whom they should elect to replace Nicholas IV. Latino Malabranca Orsini appears to be the most reasonable and spiritually minded among them. He holds up his Bible to the others and pronounces, "Whilst Christ bleeds and His holy blood waters the Holy Land—Acre and Tripoli are lost to the Infidels 'cause we hate."[3]

There were other reasons to be concerned as well. Nicholas IV had made two decisions as pope that would have a fateful effect on his Church.

On May 29, 1289, the pope had favored Charles II of

Anjou, an astute political strategist, by crowning him as the king of Sicily; he was already king of Naples. This otherwise minor figure in the history of Italy was at that time recovering from the embarrassment of losing Sicily in an important naval battle to Peter III of Aragon. But the papacy had long feuded with Aragonese rulers (before Peter III, it was his father, James I; and after Peter III, it was Peter III's son Alfonso III), and Nicholas IV was happy to restore to Charles II his Sicilian crown even if it meant little "on the ground."

Then Nicholas decreed in July 1289 that the cardinals of the Sacred College were to receive half of all the revenues accruing to the Roman See. This money, which flowed into St. Peter's Basilica from sources all over the world—from the pockets of the faithful, from the simony of civil leaders purchasing ecclesiastical offices, from the taxation of clergy and dioceses—made the Sacred College an almost independent institution. In turn, this windfall gave the cardinals, those in charge of electing a new pope, motivation to maintain position and power. Without a pope, they were accountable to no one.

By the spring of 1294 Nicholas's body had been buried at the Roman basilica of Santa Maria Maggiore for more than two years. It was more than time for the Church to move on. New leadership was desperately needed, yet no pope had been elected to replace him.

An interregnum was supposed to last only ten days. For the first nine (a novena), funeral rites would be conducted by the clergy in Rome for the deceased pope, filling the basilicas with pageantry and memories of the pope's good works. On the tenth day the Sacred College would gather and begin their work. But factions within the College were stymieing the election at every turn. There was nothing

new about this; the politics of electing a supreme pontiff
had been complicated and corrupt for centuries.

The College of Cardinals

In the eleventh century, Saint Peter Damian (ca. 1007–72),
one of the era's most influential hermits and theologians—
never known to be overly optimistic about the role of
clergy in the spiritual life of the Church—spoke of cardinals in idealized language. He expressed the view that they
might function like wise men of the empire, as an "ancient
assembly of the Romans" who, in addition to steering the
world's ship could also be "spiritual senators of the universal Church."[4] But this ideal usually went unrealized. In
the thirteenth century a cardinal was more likely to be a
scoundrel than a saint. Typically portly, political, powerful,
opinionated men, the cardinals spent most of their days
insulated from the daily lives of those whom they served.

Political motivations usually took precedence over religious and spiritual ones. Many of the cardinals inherited
their positions from members of their families, and bitter
rivalries between these families embroiled both Church
and State. This was nothing new. For centuries Scolaris,
Scottis, Pierloeonis, and Frangipanis had achieved political prominence and financial patronage through the
papacy, and had produced popes from among their numbers. Power was secured along family lines, and civil and
religious leaders relied on these family organizations for
powerful appointments, security, legal triumphs, and influence. The College of Cardinals was filled, not with the
spiritual leaders of Europe, but with its most powerful

men. It was little more than an oligarchy. Back then the questions of most importance in the room were Who are my enemies? and Who are my friends?

In response to this state of affairs, keenly felt even in the early eleventh century, an earlier pope, Nicholas II, had reformed the rules governing papal elections at a synod in 1059. Smartly, he declared a bold independence of the Church from the State, removing myriad machinations that had kept medieval popes in the pockets of Roman aristocracy and Holy Roman emperors. Future popes would be elected solely by the cardinals, he stated, and from Rome. But it took a long time—a few centuries—before this bit of wisdom would be followed. It wasn't in effect in 1292–94.

At the outset of the 1292–94 Sacred College there were only twelve members. (By contrast, today there are usually between 160 and 180.) One of the best insights into how these powerful families controlled the Church comes from Niccolò Machiavelli's famous book about politics, *The Prince*, first published in 1532. It shows that the cardinals were "strong men, who lived long, hard lives, and schemed stoutly."[5]

> To hold down the pope [the powers of Italy] made use of the barons in Rome. Since these were divided into two factions, Orsini and Colonna, there was always cause for quarrel between them; and standing with arms in hand under the eyes of the pontiff, they kept the pontificate weak and infirm. And although a spirited pope . . . sometimes rose up, still fortune or wisdom could never release him from these inconveniences. And the brevity of their lives was the cause of it; for in the ten years on the

average that a pope lived, he would have trouble putting down one of the factions. If, for instance, one pope had almost eliminated the Colonna, another one hostile to the Orsini rose up, which made the Colonna rise again, and there would not be time to eliminate the Orsini.[6]

In the election of 1292–94 it was clear from the beginning that the cardinals were in for a protracted process. The two-thirds majority required for a successful election was going to be hard to come by. The two most powerful families, the Orsinis and the Colonnas, were preventing a new pope from being crowned through deadlock after deadlock. Each family sought the man who would most likely support their interests.

The Orsini family had three representatives: Matthew Orsini was the most experienced, participating in a total of thirteen papal conclaves over a long career, including four that took place between 1276 and 1277. The Orsini family had recently produced a pope, Nicholas III (1277–80), and Matthew Orsini would later be elected pope on the first ballot on the first day of the election that was called after Celestine V's resignation. Matthew would refuse the job, and Cardinal Benedict Gaetani would be elected instead. Also present was Napoleon Orsini, nephew to Pope Nicholas III. Napoleon was the youngest member of the Sacred College, not even thirty years old at the outset. And then there was Latino Malabranca Orsini, the cardinal-bishop of Ostia and the cardinal-presider (what we call the dean today).

The Colonna family was no less influential. It was common knowledge in Rome throughout Nicholas IV's papacy that the Colonnas controlled him. Even the medieval equivalent of a comic strip remains from those days; as the *Catholic Encyclopedia* explains it: "The undue influence exercised at Rome by the Colonna . . . was so apparent . . . during [Nicholas IV's] lifetime that Roman wits represented him encased in a column—the distinctive mark of the Colonna family—out of which only his tiara-covered head emerged." The Colonnas contributed two of the cardinals in the 1292–94 Sacred College: James, one of the most powerful men in the Papal State; and his nephew, Peter, who was made cardinal by Nicholas IV in 1288 as a favor to James.

Secret Conclaves

There hadn't been a period of easy and orderly papal transition since the institution's first centuries. The very first pope was the apostle Peter, appointed by Christ when he said before others: "You are Peter, and on this rock I will build my Church, and the gates of Hades shall not prevail against it" (Mt. 16:18). Peter then appointed his successor, Saint Linus (ca. 68–79), by designating Linus to act in his place when Peter was away from Rome. Peter's appointment of Linus is attested to by at least two of the most important Latin Church Fathers, and one of the historians of that era.[7] It is also generally agreed by historians that Peter predesignated two, and perhaps three, men to follow Linus. These bishops of Rome, sitting at the epicenter and capital of the new faith, each served relatively briefly by modern standards, leading the Church up to about the year 108 C.E. For the next few centuries, with occasional interruptions when one pope simply appointed another, elections were usually held from among the Christian community of Rome, then by the clergy and bishops of Rome, and eventually—first in the year 499—by a synod of all Italian bishops at St. Peter's Basilica.

But throughout the Middle Ages papal elections were irregular and often corrupt. There were many successions by usurpers, simoniacs, and by hereditary and imperial appointments. It wasn't until the first century of the second millennium that a more orderly process was firmly established through a series of reforms. By the year 1059 the basic principles of papal elections were set in place; most important, a defined group of cardinal-electors, the Sacred College, would elect a new pope.[8] This did not solve the incidents of corruption; nevertheless, it was a step in the right direction.

The first true conclave elected Pope Gregory X in 1271. *Conclave* comes from the Latin *cum clave* and literally means "with a key," a phrase that's akin to our own "behind closed doors." Locking the doors was an emergency measure undertaken by local authorities and the people of Viterbo as a way of solving the deadlock facing the Church. Once he was elected, Gregory X then undertook to write the principle of conclave into the permanent rules of how popes are selected. He drew up a constitution called *Ubi majus periculum* and took it to the Second Council of Lyon in 1274 for formal approval. The constitution decreed that within ten days of the death of a pope all cardinals involved in papal elections should gather in the papal palace. They were to live austerely during this time. They must remain together *cum clave,* remotely, secretively, until the election came to a successful completion. They were not to receive any income or monetary support (to encourage focused listening to discern the guiding of the Holy Spirit), and local authorities were to ensure their safety and needs for provisions—food, water, and wine rations per cardinal-elector; the rations were to be reduced for each day that a protracted conclave continued.[9]

For it to be a true conclave, the cardinal-electors had to be sequestered behind doors that were locked or barred, and guarded. Conclaves usually took place in Rome or at the episcopal palace of one of the cities outside Rome, such as Perugia or Viterbo. The principles were followed fully in the election of Gregory X's successor, Innocent V, and then again for the election of Adrian V, but then Adrian decided that the special measures were no longer necessary, a decision that his successor, the Portuguese pope John XXI, reinforced. The reign of all three of these popes spanned a period of less than eighteen months. By 1292, both cardinals and ordinary citizens remembered how devastating it could be to go for months or years without a successful papal election, but locking cardinal-electors in a room and forcing them to work out their differences in a timely manner had fallen out of practice.[10]

Papal elections were once again becoming times of great commotion. Actually, *commotion* doesn't do justice to what happened. Don't imagine the simple and pious displays that were broadcast from St. Peter's in the aftermath of John Paul II's death, with nuns gathering in groups, young and old holding candlelight vigils, and teenagers kneeling silently in prayer. In the time of Peter Morrone there were *riots* in the streets, sometimes massacres, terroristic threats, and assaults upon the cardinal-electors themselves—not to mention plenty of wagering. Imagine trying to hold a papal election in the center of a bullfighting ring while a riot is going on in the stands. The cardinal-electors, who were ideally supposed to be discerning the will of God, were coming into frequent contact with the people, who were known to hold protests that would make a march on Washington seem mild mannered by comparison.

Some of the earliest papal elections are remembered for their high points of drama. In 366, for example, during the election of Pope Damasus I, some of Damasus's supporters physically attacked the supporters of a rival deacon. The violence was so widespread that soldiers were sent in by the Roman emperor. In 903 the commotion that surrounded the election of Leo V continued after he assumed the throne, and he ruled for less than three months before he was strangled by the antipope who forcibly supplanted him. And then much later, in 1378, the Roman people rioted in the streets upon the death of French-born Pope Gregory XI, screaming for the next pope to be a Roman. The cardinals elected the archbishop of Bari and fled Rome before the people heard the news, fearing for their lives because they had elected a Neapolitan.

A Boccaccian Scene

If the Sacred College had met in conclave from 1292 to 1294, not only would the election have taken less time to complete, but the cardinals might have avoided the risk of contracting the plague in Rome during those long summers. The disease was common in the late thirteenth century before reaching its high point in the early to mid-fourteenth, when the Black Death was ubiquitous. Whenever it flared, people contemplated their eternal destiny.

One might think that at times when people were faced with such calamity, the clergy might demonstrate their ability to channel God's grace, clemency, and peace in the face of near-certain death, or that at least they might offer comfort, hear confessions, and administer last rites to those on death's door. Instead, what often happened was quite the opposite: the clergy, such as the very cardinals who elected the pope, suspended all religious activity and fled to the quieter, safer countryside.[11]

Before they left Rome entirely, to get away from the clamoring crowds and the dangers of disease, the cardinals moved from the Savelli Palace to the Dominican monastery of Santa Maria sopra Minerva (later made famous by Saint Catherine of Siena, who is buried there). For weeks the Colonna family faction remained in Rome while Cardinal Benedict Gaetani retired to a villa in Viterbo to recuperate from illness. At that time Viterbo was known as "the city of popes," having in recent years witnessed the election of five popes (most recently Martin IV, in 1281), and the deaths of four. The rest of the cardinals removed to the lovely town of Rieti, a provincial capital rich with associations with the life of Francis of Assisi. It was just southwest of Rieti, near the base of the 5,575-foot Mount Terminillo, that Saint Francis dictated the Rule of his order while standing in a grove of holly trees in 1223. And it was only nine miles northwest of Rieti in Greccio where Francis celebrated Christmas with a live nativity later that same year.

Pages were running back and forth from Rome to Rieti carrying threatening letters, sometimes laced with theological arguments, from the Colonnas to the Orsinis and back again. The distance from Rieti to Rome is about fifty miles on foot through the Tiber Valley, yet the Sacred College never did gather all together in Rieti. Instead, while the streets of Rome and the Papal States filled with unrest, all the cardinal-electors made their way to Perugia, perceived to be neutral ground. It was there, removed from the clamor of ordinary life, during their third hot summer of deliberations, that the Sacred College finally seemed motivated to do something.

A MOST UNLIKELY DECISION

Few people during the Middle Ages possessed mechanical clocks. Very few ever even glimpsed one. Tolling bells tended to mark the time in and around a village. Still there was an understanding that time was connected to destiny. In that sense, Peter Morrone's letter arrived at what seemed to be a divinely appointed moment.

Everyone had something to say to the Sacred College. On the table where the mail was kept, correspondence from King Wenceslaus of Bohemia, or Edward I the King of England, or a warning note from the Grand Master of the Knights Templar about the election of a new sultan in Egypt—all would have looked vital. As would a handwritten letter from the famous octogenarian hermit of Mount Morrone, delivered on July 5, 1294.

Cardinal Latino Malabranca was a doctor of law as well as theology. Pope Nicholas III had been his uncle. In addition to his role as leader of the Sacred College, Malabranca was a fiery Dominican who also served as the

Inquisitor General, the leader of all papal inquisitions, until his death just one month after Peter's letter arrived.

Malabranca first read the letter quietly to himself. Soon afterward he announced to the others that he had received an important communiqué from one of the most holy men of the Church. He told them of its contents without naming the author.

It was well known among the members of the Sacred College that Malabranca had an affection for the teachings and personality of Peter Morrone. The annals tell us that the first cardinal in the room to respond to the letter was Cardinal Gaetani. He looked at Malabranca, smiled with a bit of a sneer, and said sarcastically, "I suppose this is one of your Peter of Morrone's visions."

There ensued some discussion of Peter the man, his views, and his reputation, until Cardinal Malabranca loudly interrupted the din to proclaim, "In the name of the Father, the Son, and the Holy Ghost, I elect Brother Peter of Morrone!"

In what happened next it seems that, despite the twenty-seven months that had passed without the election of a holy father, some of the eleven remaining cardinals (one had died of old age) must have retained hope that a good man, a truly spiritual man, could once again occupy the chair of St. Peter. There were those who said there hadn't been a holy pope since Saint Gregory the Great (590–604 C.E.), or an effective one since Innocent III (1198–1216 C.E.). Perhaps a righteous man could unite the spiritual and the temporal, bringing balance and peace to the world.

Even the cardinals of the Sacred College, men who had seen all kinds of intrigue in the halls of imperial and

religious power during the past few decades, were prepared to be inspired. That is what happened at that moment when Malabranca called out: the process of electing
a pope by inspiration.

The Latin phrase *quasi ex inspiratione* literally means
"from inspiration"; in that era it was an acceptable method
of electing a pope. It consisted of a vocal acclamation,
usually expressed in the form of a shout, just as Latino
Malabranca had done. Although it was an acceptable
method, it wasn't commonly used, so the dean's shout
probably took the other cardinals by surprise.

When we think of papal elections, we think of balloting,
the most common method, with the required two-thirds
majority to finally settle upon a name. This first and most
common way of election was most often called "scrutiny"—
secret balloting until a consensus was reached on one candidate. Ballots would be passed around and names written
down. The slips of paper from a balloting would never be
seen by anyone outside the room where the election was
held, and the cardinal-electors would keep balloting until
the necessary majority was reached.

Second, there was the delegated compromise method.
A sort of electoral college would be nominated by the
larger group of cardinals, and this group of representatives would meet to choose the man. And then there was
the third and last method, the one that Latino Malabranca
used in the summer of 1294: popular consensus that begins with one man's inspired vocal acclamation. In the
thirteenth century a saint was also sometimes declared this
way, *quasi ex inspiratione*. There were not then the involved
procedures for making saints that there are now. Saints
were often made more spontaneously.

Not long before, in the early springtime of 1294, Charles II of Naples had addressed the eleven cardinals in the papal palace in Perugia. The days were drawing longer, the nights were getting shorter, but they spent little time outside in the sun. The silk curtains hung heavily to the floor in the high-ceilinged library where they were gathered, and the beeswax candles glowed without a flicker. Charles addressed them in measured tones. He knew every man in the room personally. Some were his friends, some not. Charles was impatiently waiting to take full control of the Kingdom of Sicily, which he had lost twelve years earlier, but which had then been granted to Charles by papal decree. Now he hoped to have a new pope's assistance in order to truly take control of the island. The Sacred College must act, he told them. The continued survival of Mother Church and the security of the world—tied up as it was with the Church—depended on their wisdom and speed. Before the end of the evening, Charles clashed in fierce argument with Cardinal Gaetani, who felt that Charles was really pitching a candidate of his own choosing. Charles left dissatisfied.[1]

It was two months later that Peter wrote the letter that changed everything. He knew a few of the men meeting in the palace library and was a personal friend to at least one of them, Malabranca. The others knew him only by reputation, as the founder of a religious order, and not in the ways that they knew other powerful men—from shared days at university or casual contact in papal palaces or meetings in Rome. A hermit like Peter would rarely get to know other men in the ways that men of the world would. And he wasn't known for making public statements. But in his letter Peter told the cardinals in no uncertain terms that God could bring vengeance down upon the Church, and perhaps their houses, if they didn't act. Peter's argument convinced them whereas Charles II's had not.

Even the mostly cynical cardinals couldn't ignore that what Peter had written might be a genuine locution. These were days when God seemed to speak more freely to holy men and women in mountains or monasteries or convents than he did to others. Is this why Latino Malabranca cried out as he did?

What caused Malabranca to suggest Peter is something we will never know. Perhaps it was the Spirit of God. At least one scholar suggests that Malabranca's inspiration might have been the result of a dream he'd had, more than a response to an actual letter that he received.[2] Another offers that a general weariness and the manipulations of Charles would have reduced the cardinal-electors "to a mood susceptible to inspiration."[3] We know only that the cardinals unanimously ratified their dean's seemingly desperate suggestion. An acclamation *quasi ex inspiratione* was supposed to be ratified unanimously in order to be deemed truly inspired.

A decision by inspiration was also, by definition, unballoted. There were no actual ballots to be counted. The process was supposed to proceed like a rush of wind. We can imagine the shouts of acclamation that came forth from one cardinal after another. Cardinal Latino Malabranca called out, "In the name of the Father, the Son, and the Holy Ghost, I elect Brother Peter of Morrone!" Five of the others immediately agreed, repeating the name of Peter Morrone. *Je suis d'accord. Aio, Pietro di Morrone!* These included John Boccamazza, a cousin of Pope Honorius IV (1285–87); Gerard of Parma, the eldest member; Peter Peregrosso, the former protector of the Humiliati; Hugo

Aycelin, a French Dominican; Matthew d'Acquasparta, a Franciscan philosopher; and Benedict Gaetani, who perhaps instinctively knew how this selection would displease the Colonnas.

For their part, James Colonna and his nephew Peter Colonna wanted to pause to consider the idea, leaving this instance of *quasi ex inspiratione* short of the ideal. The Colonnas had aligned themselves with Philip the Fair, the king of France, and were seeking a pope who would unify the interests of France, Italy, and the Papal States.[4] Could the enigmatic Peter Morrone be expected to do such things? It is unclear precisely how long the dissenters held out, but it couldn't have been more than forty-eight hours.

The Spirit and the Process

It was the late-thirteenth-century theologian Giles of Rome who said that a pope either comes to the chair of St. Peter already a saint or else occupying it makes him one. But the Catholic Church has never claimed that the Holy Spirit infallibly guides the choosing of popes. If they did, they'd have to explain how God selected several men in history who even the most faithful (*especially* the most faithful) historians of the Church would call lechers, fornicators, even murderers. There are several easy examples: Pope Stephen VI (896–97), for instance, who had his predecessor's rotting corpse exhumed and put on trial; Pope John XII (955–64), who ordered the killing of people, turned the most sacred Apostolic Palace of the Lateran into a brothel, and was ultimately murdered by the husband of his mistress; and the eleventh-century Benedict IX, who sold the papacy to his godfather, Gregory VI, only to change his mind and come back and try to reclaim it.

There have been a variety of explanations over the centuries for these election mistakes. One comes from Saint James of the Marches (1391–1476), a renowned Franciscan preacher and inquisitor. He once reproached a heretic who was accused of criticizing past and present popes by saying:

> Although certain Supreme Pontiffs have died without faith, you will never find that, when one pope died in heresy, a right Catholic Pope didn't immediately succeed him. It cannot be found, in the whole series of the list of Supreme Pontiffs, that any two popes were successively and immediately heretics. Thus it cannot be said that faith has ever failed without qualification in the order of popes, since our Lord said to St. Peter, "I have prayed for you that your own faith may not fail" [Lk. 22:32]—and he said it not only for him but for the whole Church.[5]

The expectations were lower then than they are today. Apparently every *other* pope was good, and that wasn't all that bad during the Middle Ages.

The ideal of guidance by the Holy Spirit was best described in 1978 by an Italian bishop in the days leading up to the conclave that elected John Paul I: "The real protagonist [in the room] is the Other, whose presence and involvement transform the event completely and make it a community act of the Church."[6] In 1294, although there was less of this sort of idealism, in the minds of the people the answer was unequivocally yes: the Holy Spirit had guided the election of Peter Morrone. And after Peter

several other popes were elected *quasi ex inspiratione.*
Nearly four centuries after Celestine V there would be two
successive examples. The first was Cardinal Emilio Altieri,
who was elected Pope Clement X in 1670 as he was about
to turn eighty. The people outside the conclave began to
chant *"Altieri Papa!"* and the cardinals inside assented, having spent four months without coming to a decision by
scrutiny or consensus. Six years later, upon Clement X's
death, his successor was also elected by inspired acclamation. It is said that every member of that conclave kissed
Cardinal Benedetto Odescalchi's hand, and he became
Pope Innocent XI. He ruled for thirteen years fairly
successfully.

Pope John Paul II put an end to this method in 1996,
when he set out to define anew the exact election procedures or "lawful apostolic succession" for a future pope.
He titled these rules *Universi Dominici Gregis,* a Latin phrase
that means "Of the Lord's Whole Flock."[7] He specifically
cited the need to avoid any situation like the one that resulted in Celestine V's election seven hundred years ago: "I
have thus considered it fitting not to retain election by acclamation *quasi ex inspiratione,* judging that it is no longer
an apt means of interpreting the thought of an electoral
college so great in number and so diverse in origin." He
also did away with election *per compromissum,* the consensus
method. There would be no more elections in which a sort
of electoral college from among the Sacred College would
be delegated the task of choosing a new pope:

> I have therefore decided that the only form by
> which the electors can manifest their vote in the
> election of the Roman Pontiff is by secret ballot. . . .
> This form offers the greatest guarantee of clarity,

straightforwardness, simplicity, openness and, above
all, an effective and fruitful participation on the part
of the Cardinals who, individually and as a group,
are called to make up the assembly which elects the
Successor of Peter.

John Paul II then stipulated that a true conclave would
always entail the cardinal-electors remaining within Vatican City throughout the duration, ensuring their privacy
and ability to concentrate. In contrast to the commotions
of elections past, he went on to say: "I decree that the
election will continue to take place in the Sistine Chapel,
where everything is conducive to an awareness of the presence of God."[8] No more heading for the hills, from Rome
to Rieti, from Rieti to Perugia.

Secrecy would be maintained. To ensure the integrity
of the process and the election, the cardinal-electors would
each take an oath to refrain from all written communication and from consulting any media whatsoever during the
conclave. Knowing well the history of medieval papal elections, John Paul II even stipulates: "In a special way, careful and stringent checks must be made, with the help of
trustworthy individuals of proven technical ability, in order
to ensure that no audiovisual equipment has been secretly
installed in these areas for recording and transmission to
the outside." This doesn't mean that cardinals are unable
or unwilling to leak tidbits to the media, immediately before and after conclaves. It happens regardless of the rules,
as inevitably there are quotes, portions of diaries, and comments made to drivers and housekeepers from anonymous
cardinals and their aides that then find their way into the
Italian newspapers.[9]

The effect of all of the papal election reforms that have

been instituted since the summer of 1294 has been to ensure that the circumstances that conspired to elect Peter Morrone would never happen again.

Nonetheless, John Paul II made one final change that surprised observers. To the delight of some, *Universi Dominici Gregis* left open one large door of opportunity—to elect a man who shares at least one quality with our hermit pope: "Having before their eyes solely the glory of God and the good of the Church, and having prayed for divine assistance, [the cardinal-electors] shall give their vote to the person, *even outside the College of Cardinals,* who in their judgment is most suited to govern the universal Church in a fruitful and beneficial way."

SPREADING THE NEWS

As news of Peter Morrone's election spread across Italy, the responses were shock and surprise. Peter didn't at all fit the profile of a holy pontiff. For one, he was an almost complete outsider. He wasn't the son or nephew of a previous pope, or a member of the Roman curia. He was not known as a man of intellect or scholarship—or one of Plato's "philosopher kings." He was no Gregory the Great, known for his erudition and the *Commentary on Job* he wrote while he was a monk, long before he was elected (in 590 C.E.). Peter also wasn't known for drama or, particularly, passion.

Peter Morrone was an adept organizer and leader, but one whom few other men of importance had heard from in years. Among the hierarchy of the Church he had a reputation for being simpleminded. Few of his contemporaries would have ever imagined he would become pope. Every man of religious influence knew, or was soon to learn, that Peter had recently retired to a hermitage high in the mountains, dissociating himself from the daily routine of running a religious order that had preoccupied the middle part of his life.

By the time he came to write the letter to Cardinal Latino Malabranca, Peter had founded or come to control dozens of monasteries throughout the Abruzzi and Molise. He had made the Santo Spirito of Morrone, near Sulmona, the motherhouse and then had retreated once again to live as an eremite in the highest mountains overlooking the monastery. This was the setting in which he had expected to end his days.

If there had been odds-makers in thirteenth-century Europe, the chances of Peter's filling Nicholas IV's seat would have stood at about 125 to 1. Simply in terms of name recognition, the philosopher and theologian Roger Bacon would have stood at better odds of being elected, even though he too was eighty years old in the spring of 1294, was English, and had been accused of heresy two decades earlier. Raymond of Gaufredi and Etienne of Besancon, minister-general and master of the Franciscans and Dominicans, respectively, would have been clear options as well. Cardinals Matthew Orsini and James Colonna, the most powerful men of the two competing families, would have been the likely favorites.

In 490 B.C.E., according to a legend repeated by Herodotus, an Athenian man ran the 150 miles from Athens to Sparta in less than a day and a half to spread the word of the Greek victory at the battle of Marathon. But news traveled more slowly in thirteenth-century Italy than it had more than 1,500 years earlier at the height of Greek civilization. The Greeks and Romans had built a system of roads that were unrivaled until after the Renaissance. State messengers did the work of spreading news, but these roads vanished when the empire broke apart.

In thirteenth-century Italy the average man never traveled more than twenty miles from the place where he was born. A man might never visit a town five miles from his own if a mountain stood between them. News traveled as fast as a man or a horse could walk. Rarely were there roads that led directly from one city to the next, unless the distance was short. More commonly, one might journey for days around mountains before meeting up with a road that then led toward one's destination. Religious news of this sort—the election of a supreme pontiff—was more highly regarded than most news, but it never traveled fast. Word was passed along by friars walking from one city or region to another, by soldiers coming and going to and from campaigns, and by merchants making trips to sell their goods.

News would have traveled to Rome first of all the cities of Italy, for there were always travelers going to and from the Holy City. The people of Venice would have learned quickly, too, for it was the wealthiest city in all of Europe by this time, and in 1288 the city had established a coordinated plan for formal ambassadors and envoys to give and receive news from abroad.[1] But it would be weeks or months before the news reached farther-flung communes, friaries, monasteries, dignitaries, governments, and towns. It is no surprise, then, that there were no dignitaries present when Peter learned the news of his election. Few people knew of it. But it *is* surprising that none of the members of the Sacred College seem to have made plans for a quick trip to see their new leader, to bring news of God's will for the Church. Not a single cardinal joined the mission to tell Peter Morrone the news, yet at least one world leader did.

Some have suggested that Charles II visited Peter in the mountains before Peter ever wrote his fateful letter to

Cardinal Malabranca. The idea was that Charles prodded the hermit to use his spiritual authority to wake the sleeping cardinal-electors into action.[2] We know that immediately upon his ideas being rejected by the cardinals at the March meeting in Perugia, Charles then spent April 6–7 in Sulmona, below the monastery of Santo Spirito, donating fifty gold florins to support the monks' work.[3] Regardless of whether it is fact or fiction that Charles and Peter communicated before Peter wrote his letter to the Sacred College, there is no doubt that Charles was delighted by Peter's election from the moment he received the news at the palace in Melfi, which his father had taken from the German Hohenstaufen kings.

An older man is often elected pope during a time of conflict and trouble in the Church, when it is perceived that what is most needed is a man of solid reputation, one who also won't be around for very long. This thinking certainly played a part in the cardinal-electors' agreeing on Peter. Choosing Peter was also a way of steering clear of the factions that existed within the Sacred College. He was believed to have no distinct loyalties to either the Orsinis or the Colonnas.

Could he inspire the world by his moral authority? He would have to be bold. A pope could not rule with only a staff. He would need a stick. He would need to be able to wield power and influence and play a serious role in the politics of the day.

The Holy See had been a player on the world stage for centuries before the thirteenth century—since the emperor Constantine (306–12 C.E.) made Christianity the religion of the empire. Before Constantine's time, the Christian faith was outlawed and owning property or having any secular authority at all was unthinkable for

Christians. According to legend, Constantine granted Pope Sylvester I (314–35) and his successors control over the city of Rome and the western half of the Roman Empire.

The supposed Roman imperial decree known as Constantine's Donation, written sometime in the eighth century, went undetected as a fake until the early fifteenth century. Today we know that this fictional "Donation of Constantine" never actually happened. The fourth-century emperor never donated anything more than the Lateran Palace to the papacy. Yet this myth was upheld for centuries, and in 751 Saint Boniface crowned the German ruler Pepin the Short, and Pepin returned the honor by donating the lands around Ravenna to the growing papal territories. Then twenty years later Pope Adrian I (772–95) asked the emperor Charlemagne to be as virtuous as Constantine and Pepin had been and donate additional land. This included Tuscany, Lombardy, and the island of Corsica. By 1054, Pope Leo IX was using the Constantine Donation to bolster his claims for controlling vast swaths of land. "[I]n a letter of 1054 to Michael Cærularius, Patriarch of Constantinople, he cites the 'Donatio' to show that the Holy See possessed both an earthly and a heavenly *imperium,* the royal priesthood."[4] By the time of Pope Gregory VII (1073–85) the papacy had begun to define itself by the territory of the Papal States, calling these lands its divine inheritance, *terra sancti Petri,* or "the sacred land of Peter."

The Habsburg monarch Rudolf I would donate all of Romagna to the Holy See in 1278, by which time the Donation was widely acknowledged and became the basis for Church authorities to add future landholdings. Henceforth the largest landholder in all of Italy would be whoever was pope, and he could presume all manner of power, including taxation and commanding armies. For most of three-quarters of a millennium the lands of the Papal States encompassed much of what is present-day Italy. Today Vatican City is all that is left of this medieval theocracy.

The modern notion of a pope who is only, or even primarily, a spiritual leader would have been completely foreign to the understanding of people of Peter Morrone's day. The pope was the chief spiritual authority of the Church, but since a few centuries before Peter Morrone the bishop of Rome had also been the world's most powerful Christian—if not, also, the world's most powerful man.

Did the cardinals who elected Peter believe that the hermit pope would understand these distinctions? Did they believe that he would be able to rule with the strong and certain hand that would be required? How would he relate to world leaders?

Much of the surprise at Peter's election centered on the fact that no one knew him to be even an observer of world events. He was certainly no Leo the Great, the early pope who not only met Attila face-to-face in 452, but then somehow convinced the Hun not to invade Italy. Peter was shut away in his hermitage. One of our great novelists, Cormac McCarthy, wrote in *Blood Meridian or The Evening Redness in the West:* "The man who believes that the secrets of this world are forever hidden lives in mystery and fear." This would seem to characterize Peter. What he desired to know, and knew most deeply, with the greatest certainty, was what he learned in prayer. The affairs of the world had never much concerned him.

There have been many who believed that the election of Peter Morrone was nothing less than a miracle. It had the stuff of divine inspiration. Even the name that Peter took for himself as pope, Celestine, suggests that he believed celestial powers had guided the cardinal-electors. As a star led wise men to the Son of God in Bethlehem 1,300 years earlier, divine intelligence could have led the College of Cardinals to choose him. Like a divining rod, the Holy Spirit pointed them toward the man destined to lead the Church out of its corruption and compromises, and into a new era. Hope was discovered as one might find treasure buried in a field.

Did the cardinals believe that this hermit wouldn't be a nuisance as so many of his predecessors were? It would be easy to pull the strings of an octogenarian pope, and his reign wouldn't last very long anyway. Inspiration may have guided the Sacred College, but so did the idea among some of them that they were buying time until they could each gather the wherewithal to get their own man in.

But he would puzzle them. Devout and introverted, Peter Morrone was also strident and charismatic. Known to be short-tempered, he came with all of the trappings of a man who was meek. The man who would be crowned Pope Celestine V was one of the greatest bundles of contradictions that the world has ever seen.

THEY CAME TO TAKE HIM AWAY

Each hermit believed he was *solus cum solo,* or alone with the alone. The only relationship that truly mattered was that between a hermit and his God. Everything else was expendable in a life designed to expend.

Before Peter Morrone became pope, he lived as a contemplative, engaging in the most passionate life available to a man: a solitary life in the mountains. From Plato to Plotinus to Jerome to Peter Damian to Thomas Aquinas to Dante, nearly every significant spiritual and philosophical thinker of the Christian era had written or preached the value of the contemplative life over the active life.

Then (as now) it seemed to be universally agreed that the more a man was able to live every moment of earthly existence as a gift from the Creator, the higher spiritual state he would achieve. Fishermen may make good disciples, but they don't make good contemplatives. The active life gets in the way. Just as one can't truly appreciate the paintings of a museum by sprinting through its corridors, one cannot know God and truth in wage earning and domestic business. That's why Christ asked his fishermen apostles to leave their nets and follow him. He wanted a higher life for them. Despite the fact that it was a fisherman, Saint Peter, who was given the keys to the kingdom by Christ, the values of stillness, silence, and contemplation took hold of the Christian imagination during the Middle Ages. As one of the most popular poets of the late Middle Ages would summarize it, "Every anchorite or hermit, monk or friar, if he follows the way of perfection is on a level with the twelve apostles."[1]

Many great thinkers have written that the heart seeks after that which it loves, and the most proper love of all is love of God, but the heart needs time, space, and quiet in order to nurture such love. Since the true purpose of life is to prepare for life after death, serious Christians saw the earthly trappings—domestic duties, family, houses, wage earning—as obstacles, whereas the monastic life, and especially the eremitic life, was the school of heaven. "O taste and see that the Lord is good," the psalmist sang in Psalm 34:8. A man needs time in order to love God properly and fully. For the one who is able to devote time to contemplation, the reward is great. He can be truly happy, for contemplation "is more enjoyable than any other human pleasure. Spiritual enjoyment surpasses bodily enjoyment, . . . and the love with which we love God in charity surpasses every love," said Thomas Aquinas.[2] "In addition, how many greater gifts will come to you in the truly blessed life that lies before us, is, I must admit, beyond my capacity to discuss. . . . Therefore, hide this treasure, namely Christ . . . in the receptacle of your heart. With it in your possession cast away all concern for anything else in this world," wrote Peter Damian.[3] Contemplation is the best of all ways of living.

The contemplative life also opens a person up to seeing God in ways that are usually hidden from others. The contemplative's experience of God is direct and it's as if he's already living in heaven.

Hearing Voices

Peter Morrone was "betrothed" to God, and it was his aim to spend every waking hour of every day in the presence of Christ; he spoke with him, and often heard Christ's voice in response.

He lived during the Ptolemaic era when the earth was believed to be at the center of the universe, with the moon, sun, stars, and other planets revolving around it. Hell was located in the deepest recesses of the earth, and heaven, high above our heads beyond the sky. That is why mountains were so important—divine proximity was taken very seriously.

In the fifth century, Saint Ambrose of Milan claimed that Jesus Christ was crucified on the same hill where the first man, Adam, had long ago been buried. Throughout the Middle Ages Christians sought out places made sacred by association. The height of Peter's mountains was not accidental. He sought the highest mountaintop he could climb because he desired to be near his Creator. He wanted his prayers to be spoken and whispered closely into the ear of God.

People in the thirteenth century had no understanding whatsoever of the composition of the atmosphere. It wasn't until the early sixteenth century that Leonardo da Vinci began to experiment with how air is consumed during combustion, and not until the late eighteenth century that oxygen was identified. In Peter's time, the atmosphere of earth was a place for winds and spirits, not a layer of gases retained by the planet's gravity.

Hearing voices in the wind and woods was a common experience among Christian mystics according to medieval chronicles and tales. We read of ordinary men and women having divine experiences causing them to fall upon the ground, become frozen in fear; sometimes they meet inexplicable strangers in lonely places or feel ravished in ecstasy. As his Autobiography makes clear again and again, Peter experienced these things. God surely speaks to all men and women, but to some, divine stimuli are more readily received.

One of the most common diagnoses of that era (continuing up until the nineteenth century) was "brain fever," a pseudo-medical explanation for a rise in body temperature brought on, it was believed, by an overexcitement of the senses. This was a kind of ailment that assailed a sensitive soul who took in more than he could handle. Since ancient Mesopotamian times, human beings have acknowledged fevers, occasions when the body's internal temperature rises beyond what is normal, but it wasn't until very recently that we knew why body temperature rises and that this process is actually good for us. Medieval people feared the fever, and the remedy for "brain fever" was to cut back on stimuli.

There is a type of overstimulation that can occur in men and women like Peter who spend long periods of time alone with God. Figures dance and voices speak to a live imagination in quiet places. He also practiced extreme fasting and other ascetic behaviors, which brought on mystical experiences.

From his grotto, Peter Morrone prayed the Psalms with punctual regularity, structuring his day with set times of prayer as he moved through the Psalter, genuflecting as well, at least five hundred times a day to his God.[4] He prayed the liturgical hours of Compline, Vigils, Matins, Prime, Terce, Sext, None, and Vespers. He would have known the entire Psalter from memory, and the words of the Psalms would have sprung to his mind and his lips with ease, and whether he was experiencing moments of pain or joy, boredom or dread, he would be able to express his feelings with a psalmist's intensity.

When he was composing his letter to Cardinal Latino Malabranca in June 1294 he could have easily heard these words from Psalm 12 in his ears: "Help, Lord; for there is no longer any one who is godly; for the faithful have vanished from among the sons of men. Everyone utters lies to his neighbor; with flattering lips and a double heart they speak." As he stood on the mountain mourning the sorry state of his blessed Holy and Catholic Church he might have prayed: "Consider and answer me, O Lord my God; lighten my eyes, lest I will sleep the sleep of death" (Ps. 13:3). And he might have remembered the words of the prophet Isaiah to whom he had been compared: "They shall not hurt or destroy in all my holy mountain; for the earth shall be full of the knowledge of the Lord as the waters cover the sea" (Is. 11:9).

Along Came the World to Peter's Doorstep

Peter did not exactly live alone. He was not entirely solitary or reclusive. He had retreated to his remote location but there were other men nearby, all living as hermits. Mostly they spent their days alone, eating, praying, working, or sleeping, but they would still see one another from time to time and gather as a community to pray at least once each day. They formed a loosely organized cluster of individual hermitages on the eastern edge of Mount Morrone, along the Sulmona basin.

The community was accustomed to pilgrims visiting their holy mountains. It was nearly a daily occurrence for Peter and his brothers to see strangers on the hillsides, seeking out the huts and caves where hermits made their rough homes among the trees. For the medieval man and woman, a walking pilgrimage was like a dream holiday vacation is to us. People undertook them as a form of therapy, or to escape their debts and debtors, or to enjoy life by getting away from domestic responsibilities, and occasionally even for spiritual reasons. One pilgrimage to Compostela or Jerusalem, or receiving a face-to-face blessing from a holy hermit, could save a person several years in purgatory. But Peter never could have imagined encountering the visitors that hiked up the mountain to see him in the summer of 1294.

Artists have given us an idea, however. A sixteenth-century fresco depicting the scene hangs on the walls of the Gallery of Maps in the Vatican (on the vault corresponding to the frescoed map of Abruzzo). It is entitled *The Hermit St. Peter of Morrone Receiving the News of His Election to the Papacy*. Noblemen are shown atop noble steeds, led by native guides on foot, pointing the way around turns and through underbrush, steeply climbing up the mountain, ascending the psalmist's hill of the Lord to find the holy one. And there kneels Peter on the ledge beyond their immediate vision, pleading with God, oblivious to their coming.

Meanwhile, the king of Naples was on his way to Mount Morrone as well. We don't know from whom he received the news about the new pope at the palace at Melfi, and so rapidly, but together with his son, Charles Martel of Anjou, Charles II quickly traveled to Sulmona. There, to the foot of Mount Morrone, was as far as Charles II would go. His lameness made mountain climbing an impossibility; but he sent his royal son up the peak to try to reach the hermit before the ecclesiastical entourage could arrive.

Toward the top of these mountains, the quiet of beech trees and mountain pine recedes as you climb beyond 3,000 feet, where the dwarf junipers and wildflowers grow. At 5,000 feet, just under the clouds, songbirds become fewer and ravens and hawks more common, their calls starting to sound plaintively human as they move in their slow, winding circles. It was under such a canopy that delegates of the Sacred College made their way upward to inform Peter of what the cardinals had done.

A group of men—priests, soldiers, and their attendants—had assembled in Perugia on July 11 to make the trip to carry the news. The troop was led by the French archbishop of Lyon, Bérard of Got (brother of Raymond of Got, who later became Pope Clement V), wearing the full regalia of his priestly office, and neither the archbishop nor those who accompanied him were accustomed to mountain climbing, especially in the heat of a July afternoon. The journey took them at least ten days.

When they reached the top of the mountain, they found a simple hermitage with two small chambers. A small opening served as a window. One of the most important witnesses to these events, James Stefaneschi (ca. 1270–1343), who was the son of a Roman senator, and who would later become a cardinal, peered inside Peter's hermitage and saw an "unkempt, blear-eyed recluse, peering in bewilderment at such unwonted company on his little plateau."[5]

According to legend, a friend and fellow friar by the name of Roberto had hurried ahead of the entourage, to tell Peter who was coming to fetch him. As a result, Peter was prepared to turn the party of visitors away before they ever arrived at the top. Surely they must be joking, he thought. Peter wasn't very trusting by nature, and when the group of clergy reassured him it was no joke he did the one thing any normal, solitary hermit would have done. He refused the job.

As one scholar has put it, "To characterize the choice [of Peter as pope] as eccentric is probably an understatement."[6] Peter wasn't the first man to want to avoid the chair of St. Peter, to realize immediately that what it demanded was not for him. He also wouldn't be the first pope to pine for the life he had left behind, to spend his time wallowing in self-pity over what he was missing. But he *was* the first to attempt to *run* from the honor. He resisted the call of the cardinals at first. *Resisted* may even be too simple a word. Peter seems to have actually hid himself from his approaching visitors. The Roman poet Petrarch says that Peter tried taking to his heels. The old *Catholic Encyclopedia* talks about how "Pietro heard of his elevation with tears"— but even this traditionalist source didn't mean tears of *joy*. They continue, "but, after a brief prayer, obeyed what seemed the clear voice of God"!

The entourage would have dragged Peter to Rome and

strapped the crozier into his right hand if necessary. But Peter happened to be residing within the territory of the House of Anjou, ruled by Charles II. Kings traveled well, and the two Charleses made better time than the archbishop and the others. Before Peter could refuse the will of the election, Charles Martel was the one who brought the hermit assurances from his father that his monks, his hermitage, and the future of his order would be safe.

Finally, Peter told those gathered, "I accept."

The distinguished retinue began to chant, *"Viva il papa!"* "Long live the pope!" For those votaries, nobles, and churchmen who had made the journey, there was enthusiasm for the future. The official decision of the Sacred College was read aloud to Peter and all of his brothers who gathered around. Petrarch later tells us: "The ragged, haggard, trembling hermit, fleeing in terror from the proffered honor, then bowing to what he held to be a celestial command, then descended from Mount Morrone."

All the while, thousands of people had gathered around the bottom of Mount Morrone. Many had watched the finely clothed churchmen awkwardly making their way through the oaks and maples, so they were surprised to see the twenty-two-year-old Charles Martel, a young layman, descending at the hermit's side. Others were there as well. It has been suggested that Giovanni Pipino, a resident of nearby Barletta, was present. He would later become famous for building the great church of San Pietro of Maiella in Naples.[7] Once the entourage arrived in Sulmona, Charles Martel and Charles II arranged to have Peter consecrated within their realm.

All that Peter had done to deserve this honor was to write to the cardinal-electors, offering them an apocalyptic vision of what God might allow to happen if they didn't elect a holy pontiff, and soon. He was never expecting that he would be asked to do what he was now charged with doing. This is not to say that he wasn't a man of ambition. The early chroniclers might have us believe that Peter was guileless and simple, but the events of a life spanning more than eight decades tell a different story.

PART II
PETER OF MORRONE, 1209–93

Peter Morrone . . . we will see, perhaps, at last achieved

What in the cell of your heart you truly believed.

And if all the world was being deceived,

Many a curse will follow after you.

—JACOPONE OF TODI,
"Epistle to Pope Celestine V"

NOW I WILL TELL YOU OF MY LIFE

As with many of the saints, we know very little about the early years of Peter Morrone. What we do know comes from a number of texts that, for better or worse, are considered by modern readers as hagiography. In other words, these sources have devotional value, offering insight into the contemporary or near-contemporary perspective of Peter's personality and influence, but they add little to what we know for certain about the man's life. One of these is an Autobiography, supposedly written by Peter himself, though strangely it fluctuates back and forth from third-person narrative ("He often saw these and other good things in visions") to first-person ("I will first say something about my parents"). This suggests that it was written by many people, and not necessarily even by Peter. Still, tradition holds that this is Peter's story of his life. Intriguingly, the earliest extant manuscript of the Autobiography resides in the Vatican Archives and dates to about a generation after Peter's death. An anonymous archivist long ago marked on the outside of the text that it was written in Peter's own hand.[1]

There is also the *Opus Metricum* of James Stefaneschi, one of the men who visited Peter on Mount Morrone. The *Opus* is a biographical poem written in dactylic hexameter (an homage to Homer and Virgil), the first part of which was composed in 1296, the year of Peter's death, and the third and final part was finished in 1319. Stefaneschi, who was held in high regard by Peter while he was pope, and who was made a cardinal-deacon by the next pope, sent the work to the monks of Santo Spirito near Sulmona, the motherhouse of Peter's religious order. The work describes the coronation of Celestine V, his abdication, his canonization, and the miracles that occurred on the way to his canonization. One of Peter's monastic disciples, Thomas of Sulmona, also wrote a short Life of him relatively soon after his death, sometime between 1300 and 1305. Both the 1319 version of Stefaneschi's poem and the Life penned by Thomas make reference to some autobiographical writings of Peter that as of today have never been found.

All of these texts fit the definition of medieval hagiography in almost every way. They consist of narrative or verse without reference to historical evidence. But there's an old Italian saying that goes, *Una bugia ben detta val più di un fatto stupido,* or "A lie well told is worth more than a stupid fact."[2] In the Middle Ages these narratives were the essence of good storytelling, and the approximation to fact was rarely of much concern to those who either told the tales or listened to them. Still, these spiritual portraits serve an important purpose even today, because they etch into history the lives of great men and women and honor their earthly existence, proclaiming their role as agents in salvation history. While the facts may sometimes be in question, hagiography serves to create a truth that transcends specific day-to-day actions and occurrences—that truth being that all Christians are called to sainthood, even reluctant ones like Peter Morrone.

Peter begins the story of his life in his Autobiography, as any good son would, by mentioning his parents: "My father was named Angelerio, a God-fearing, humble man. My mother was Maria, a saint in my life. Together they had twelve sons, but mother raised me almost entirely on her own, since my father died when I was just a boy."[3]

Peter was born in Molise in 1209, the same year that Francis of Assisi was gathering his first followers in nearby Umbria. It was on April 16 of that year that Saint Francis, Bernard of Quintavalle, and Peter Catani opened the Scriptures together at the home of their local bishop and found the words in the Gospels that would inspire the creation of the Franciscan order. Less than a year later, the first twelve Franciscans would walk to Rome to visit Pope Innocent III. Also in the spring of 1209, that same pope recruited more than 10,000 men to raid the mountainous regions of southern France to root out the Cathar heretics in what became known as the Albigensian Crusade. That October, he crowned the Bavarian Otto IV as Holy Roman Emperor ("Roman Catholic King") in Rome. Halfway around the world, 1209 was also the year in which Beijing was being marauded by the Mongol leader Genghis Khan. This was the year when Peter was born.

There was little guarantee that Peter, one of twelve children—all of them boys—would survive past infancy. At this time throughout Europe only half of all children survived to the age of five. Only one in four people saw the age of forty. There were no vaccines or antibiotics, let alone an understanding of how to kill ordinary contagions. In the minds of medieval people, death was determined wholly by God, not by disease.

Peter's father's name, Angelerio, or "little angel," was once a common name in Italy but is no longer. "When my father died of old age, I was but five or six. My mother still had seven sons," Peter tells us. Five of the twelve had died. His mother was named Maria, in honor of the Blessed Virgin. Yet the hagiographers don't draw direct comparisons to Christ, the Lord of angels, in the earliest biographies of Peter. Instead, they turn to the Old Testament story of Joseph, the son of Jacob, and establish parallels that might help explain how an ordinary boy could grow up to become pope.

Peter was the favorite of his parents (or at least of his mother) and was looked on with suspicion by his brothers. Although his siblings rejected the idea of dedicating one's life to God, Peter from a very early age embraced it. When his mother sent Peter off to study—presumably, as was the custom, promising him to the monastery while he was still a boy—the Autobiography says that the other brothers were tempted by the devil to do what they could to prevent Peter from focusing on his studies. Later Maria sold some of the family property in order to pay a teacher for Peter's instruction, and it's said that this was done contrary to the desires of his brothers, as well. When Peter begins to see visions, he tells only his mother about them. She instructs him to keep the information to himself, but the devil tempts Peter and he blurts out his experiences while playing with his siblings. The other children threaten to hit him, but, the text says, angels protect him.

Mother and child are described as having much in common, including vivid nighttime dreams, which they share with each other in the mornings. One evening Maria dreamed that Peter was a shepherd of sheep, and according to the Autobiography, this saddens her. Presumably, the vision of her son engaged in an ordinary occupation is dissatisfying to her. The next day, while standing with Peter, who is twelve, Maria says to him, "Last night I dreamed about a man of God," and Peter quickly responds as if to interpret her vision, "He will be a shepherd of souls." "It is you!" she tells him, with joy.

San Angelo Limosano

Peter grew up in the small village of San Angelo Limosano in the most remote part of Italy, a region Peter knew as Abruzzi e Molise, home to the highest peaks of the Apennines and populated by some of the most fiercely independent Italians.[4] His village, located in the diocese of Sulmona, is about 115 miles east of Rome. To the immediate east of San Angelo Limosano, the Abruzzi town of Isernia is the site of what is perhaps the oldest-known human settlement on the European continent. Scientists date it to sometime around 700,000 B.C.E. Around 295 B.C.E., Isernia and all of Molise fell into the hands of the Romans. All of what we call "Italy" today came under nominal Roman control at about that time.

The Romans finally subdued the people of Molise in the Social War of 91–88 B.C.E., bringing them under the control of the empire so they could tax the people and enlist the men in the Roman army. But it was a notoriously bitter struggle and the people of these rugged areas remained only begrudgingly Roman for centuries. The German king Frederick II Hohenstaufen (r. 1220–50) was the first ruler to unite these lands since the fall of the Roman Empire, only to then see the territory fall into disarray with the advent of Charles I and Charles II.

Molise, then as today, is a mostly rural, undistinguished area with little of interest. The terrain is rough with craggy mountains, the cities and towns full of dark streets. For millennia it has been home to both solitaries and outlaws.

The areas of Molise and Abruzzo are prone to tremors and earthquakes. The region of Peter's birth has almost literally been held together by scaffolding, since long ago; towns have sprung up from where mountains and valleys came together along fault lines. The first recorded earthquake happened there in 1315, but the fault lines are ancient. For years and years, nuns and monks have recited daily prayers for the safety of town and citizenry, particularly in the month of January, since the saying goes, "When the cold is at its greatest, the earthquake is at its strongest."[5] It is recorded that a quake in 1349 left more than 800 people dead. In the last century alone, a 1915 earthquake killed more than 30,000. A tremor in 1980 nearly leveled San Angelo Limosano, and there are hundreds of people who still live in temporary shelters that were erected in desperation in the aftermath of that event. Similarly, long-lasting effects will surely be felt after the quake that struck L'Aquila, the capital city of Abruzzo just to the north of San Angelo Limosano, in 2009, killing several hundred and leaving approximately 65,000 homeless.[6]

Peter knew warmth and cold, hot sunshine and bitter

winter winds, since he lived in one of a few places in temperate Italy that consistently sees snowfall. In the valleys surrounded by mountains, it's not uncommon for snow to fall for days and weeks on end.

In Peter's era people understood the world around them through allegory, symbolism, and parallels that might seem far-fetched to us today. Medieval people were continually seeking lines of connection between the natural and the divine. The outward appearances of things were believed to cloak deeper, spiritual realities. This was even true of the topography of a place. The hills that separate the Molise and Abruzzo from the plains and the cities of Rome and Naples, the Abruzzi mountains to the east that slope down toward the lonely shores of the Adriatic Sea— these geographical features establish the region's sense of independence from Rome.

The twentieth-century Italian novelist Ignazio Silone, who grew up in the Abruzzi, offers some descriptions of life in a remote village that give us an idea of what Peter's experience might have been like. Same as Peter, Silone lost four siblings and his father to illness before he turned thirteen. In *Fontamara* (1930) Silone describes "an old and obscure village of poor farmers . . . in a valley halfway between the hills and the mountains.

"Most of the doors and windows of the houses are clearly visible from the plain: a hundred little huts almost all on the same level—irregular, unformed, blackened by time and worn down by wind, rain and fire." A church sits at the center of all things: "The upper part of Fontamara is dominated by the church with its tower and the terraced square, reached by a steep road that goes through the entire village and is the only one over which carts can pass. . . . To an observer . . . the village looks like a herd of dark sheep, and the church tower like a shepherd. It is, in short, a village like so many others, but the universe to those who grow up there."[7]

At the center of life, especially during Peter's days, was church. Public ritual was central to the life of the people and bound the village together. Processions and parades, marked by candle lighting, bell ringing, the wafting of incense, and the sprinkling of holy water, occurred during every calendar month and usually began at the church. Among the most important celebrations were the Annunciation (March 25), the birth of John the Baptist (June 24), the Assumption of the Blessed Virgin Mary (August 15), and the Feast of Saint John the Evangelist (December 27). These rituals of Italian village life formed Peter as a man of God.

At minimum, he and his family would have received Holy Communion at the parish church on the three traditional days of the year: Christmas, Easter, and Pentecost. They would have gone to confession more frequently according to the stirrings of their consciences—at least once a year, as mandated by the Fourth Lateran Council (1215), but it was also common for the most sincere penitents to confess to their priests once a month or, occasionally, weekly. Confession was penance but it was also the only time in a Christian's life when he would be able to obtain spiritual counsel from someone with recognized spiritual wisdom and religious authority, although some local priests, then as now, found their parishioners' enthusiasm for confession disturbing to their other duties and leisure.[8]

It wasn't until the sixteenth century that the confessional box, containing a partition separating priest and penitent, was created. In the thirteenth century, a sinner confessed to his priest face-to-face.[9] The earnest faithful of this era asked much of their priests, as do their counterparts today, and their priests often rebuffed or avoided them. If Peter was one of these earnest penitents while young, in later life he would experience the phenomenon from the other side.

7

I BECAME A MAN
WHEN I BECAME A MONK

Miracles abound in the early hagiographical texts about
Peter. There are inexplicable healings, a malevolent devil,
protective angels and saints, enlightening visions, and so-
lutions to problems that defy rational explanations. For example, there is a story in which Peter's mother sends him
to find grain in the fields even though it is well after har-
vest time. The boy protests, but something moves him and
he does what his mother says. Then, as divine providence
would have it, the boy, like the Hebrew Joseph before him,
finds grain abundant enough to feed his starving family.
Another story tells of when Peter, in need of religious instruction, receives help directly from the Blessed Mother
and Saint John the Beloved, both of whom pick up a copy
of the Psalter and sing David's songs sweetly to him. It is a
most blessed and intimate kind of instruction, almost like
mother's milk.

There are other wonders that Peter experienced in
early childhood, which also set the young boy apart, like
Moses in the basket or young Samuel in the Temple. For

example, Peter shows a devotion to Mother Church as a boy. He experiences dreams and undergoes temptations in the form of visions. He is tormented by demons and battles with the devil almost constantly. He experiences frequent nightmares. Before he becomes a teenager, a vision tells him of his future, and everyone around him acknowledges that he will grow up to be a religious man. All of the miraculous happenings described are sure signs of God's favor, and that makes sense because hagiographical literature shows the patterns of how an ordinary man is transformed into a saint.

All the while, it is clear that Peter lacks the family heritage, connections, and influence that previous popes of his time enjoyed. In thirteenth-century Italy, to be born poor was to remain poor. There was no public schooling, so a boy from Peter's background would usually remain illiterate throughout life. In contrast, consider one of the popes who lived in the century before him: Lotario dei Conti of Segni, who became Pope Innocent III (b. 1160). Like many young men from wealthy and influential families, Lotario was sent to Paris to study. Given the freedom to learn in a leisurely fashion, he became an intellectual. For close to a decade Lotario studied logic, classical literature, rhetoric, law, and theology. From young adulthood on, he could quote effortlessly from Ovid and Horace as easily as from Aristotle and Saint Jerome, and this wide learning was evident in his eloquent homilies, messages, and voluminous correspondence.

Or consider Peter in contrast to another pontiff who preceded him: Nicholas III, who ruled from 1277 to 1280. Nicholas is most remembered for his nepotism. He was an Orsini; his election was the work of political maneuvering, and his pontificate, likewise. Because of his connections

Nicholas had ample opportunity to grant favors to famous friends and to make friends famous. His father was a personal friend of Francis of Assisi, and Nicholas later wrote in a papal bull about his personal knowledge of the Rule of Saint Francis and his familiarity with the intentions of its famous author (using the royal "We" that was until very recently characteristic of how popes referred to themselves): "We, who from tender years have aroused our affections for the Order itself, by growing up during those years with some of the companions of the same Confessor, to whom his life and comportment were known, have discussed in frequent conversation the very rule and holy intention of blessed Francis himself."[1] This is another way of saying: My dad introduced me to the source of it all.

Peter had no such experience. Peter's family struggled to make ends meet. His parents were not wealthy and they weren't intellectuals or favorites in the royal court. His father undoubtedly worked very hard and long all of his days, until he died, long before Peter reached adolescence. After a father died it was common for the mother to enter a convent, sending the children off to monasteries or to live with relatives. Another renowned religious figure, Guibert of Nogent (ca. 1055–1124), lived that kind of life. Born in northern France, Guibert was thrust into the monastery at the tender age of twelve, following the death of his father, several years of private tutoring, and his mother's departure to a convent. Peter was not separated from his mother; she stayed put, presumably aided by surrounding family, and Peter lived out his youthful days among family until he was permitted to pursue his monastic vocation.

Popes, cardinals, archbishops, bishops, even priests, were, then as now, men of a close fraternity. Just as the teenagers who attend Eton and Harrow are the ones most naturally destined to become the leaders in the Church of England and members of Parliament, so the young men who studied in Paris during Peter's day were the ones most geared to take on leadership and influence in Church and State. Relationships kindled in those formative days were the girders that built their future power.

> The products of these schools formed an international society, men who literally spoke the same language (Latin), knew the same literature, valued the same intellectual skills. Having spent five to ten years together in the same schools, following the same curriculum, absorbing the same ideas, they knew one another well. A bishop in Scotland might feel closer to a bishop in Sicily or Germany, men he had spent his adolescence and youth with in school, than to the local clergy and laity, who had never been far from home."[2]

Economically, intellectually, and religiously, Peter was an outsider. He had no patron, no famous relatives, no dowry. He owned no land in a time when landownership was a prerequisite for every sort of power.

On paper, Peter may not have looked impressive, but it has been borne out throughout history that the outsider living free of the norm can develop a strength that people "on the inside track" have difficulty matching.

From his earliest days as an adult (when one feels things most acutely) Peter probably experienced his lack of opportunities, and no doubt he realized that those who enjoyed the privileges of wealth and education were more likely to fall into leadership positions within the

Church. He must have seen the need to make his own way, and because he followed his own path, he grew into someone who felt most comfortable existing on the outside looking in.

Peter entered the Benedictine order when he was seventeen, and within the span of just a few years he seems to have been transformed from a boy devoted to his mother to a fiercely independent young man. Independence agreed with him, and his natural intellect began to blossom. As the second youngest in his family, he had the opportunity to follow a religious vocation because he had older brothers who remained at home to see that his mother was taken care of. He was committed to the monastery according to the rules laid out in chapter fifty-nine of the Benedictine Rule: Parents promise a boy to a monastery while "the child is still of tender age," and they agree "under oath" never to give the boy any of their property, so that he will rely solely on the graces of the place to which he is bound.

Peter's monastery, Santa Maria, was located in Faifula, a short southeasterly journey from San Angelo Limosano, and just to the north of the ancient city of Benevento. With a Roman theater built by the emperor Hadrian and a single barrel-vaulted white marble arch built by Trajan, Benevento and the surrounding area are full of reminders of the Roman past. The powerful Christian structures and symbols were usually built alongside, or literally on top of, what had been Roman or pagan sites—as in the case of the Convent of Sant'Agostino, underneath which was recently discovered the remnants of a first-century temple to Isis.[3] Faifula lay in the picturesque countryside of Montagano along the road to Rome. This land of farms and pinewoods was owned by successive feudal lords, some of whom sent a portion of their yield each year to the monastery as tithe and support. In exchange, daily Masses were said by the monks for their patrons.

We don't know much about Peter's time in Faifula, but it seems apparent from his Autobiography that the young man was almost immediately drawn to a love of solitude. Most monks were not; they enjoyed community life and the security of the cloister. For Peter, a yearning for greater solitude was combined with a desire for monastic reform. By Peter's day, many monasteries had lost their spiritual luster. Many religious communities throughout the Western Church had degenerated from centers of civilization, sacrifice, hospitality, and redemption into the largest land-holders and power brokers in their region. Many men (and later women) who joined communities for purely unselfish reasons, as a way of embracing life, began to despair when they saw that the life they were being asked to live was not what they thought it should be. Monasteries had become places that a true Christian heart despised. That is why so many spiritual movements were popping up in the days of Peter's spiritual formation. That is why so many young men like Peter didn't stay within the cloister for long. A different sort of life called him.

He shows his predilection in the pages of the Autobiography when he reflects, "As a child I desired more and more for God, and more and more to find a place of hermitage." One imagines that those mysterious places in the mountains drew the imagination of Peter as they have sparked the minds of many of every age. He knew that a hermit had far greater autonomy than did a monk living in a monastery. There was more time to pray and less need for the human conversation and negotiation that are part of living closely in community with other men.

The allure of religious life was strong, not only for spiritual reasons, and the monastery was seen as a place of security, but also as a place of refuge. A twelfth-century monk once wrote: "This whole world is a place of exile; and so long as we live in this life we are pilgrims to the Lord; therefore we need spiritual stables and inns, and such resting-places as monasteries afford to us. Moreover, the end of all things is at hand, and the whole world is seated in wickedness; therefore it is good to multiply monasteries for the sake of all who would flee from the world in order to save their souls."[4] For men like Peter, the hermitage became the best chance of surviving the pilgrimage.

At the age of twenty, probably in the year 1230, Peter left his monastery at Faifula and took to the life of a solitary. The Autobiography states that he did this on his own initiative, without sanction from any abbot or bishop, and there is no reason to doubt on that point. As Peter tells it, "There was no servant of God in my region with whom to consult." So he took his religious life into his hands, just as earlier prophetic figures had done. In this we see the early signs of his later personality. He was a man who could be determined and aloof at the same time. After three years of living as Brother Peter Angelerio, Benedictine community monk, Peter went on to become a hermit of the nearby mountains, a man in search of salvation and anxious to bring God's kingdom into a fractured world.

A HERMIT LOVES HIS CAVE

As a Benedictine at Faifula Peter had discovered the writings of Peter Damian (ca. 1007–72), a spiritual ascetic and theologian who would influence Peter's thought in a variety of ways for the rest of his life.

Born to a poor family in Ravenna, Damian exhibited an exceptional intelligence from an early age. So much so that his older brother, a local priest, removed the young orphan from his life of poverty and had him educated in theology and canon law. Damian made such remarkable progress that by the time he was twenty-five years old he was already a renowned professor in Parma. But soon this intelligent man felt called by God to leave behind the life of an academic and to turn his focus to the inner life. He departed for the Marches, where he joined an eremitic monastery famed for its austerities.

There Damian became a profound teacher and writer on the spiritual life. His writings inspired ascetics in middle to late medieval times. He became a theologian, a poet, and an expert biblical exegete; some referred to him, even in his own lifetime, as a new Jerome, and he was regarded popularly as a saint even before his death in the Italian province where he was born.

Depending on your perspective, Peter Damian's writings reveal either a tremendous pessimism or a radical honesty about the state of the Catholic Church in his time. He was a zealot for reform, urging greater seriousness of purpose and penitence, calling for a revival of solitude and poverty as supreme virtues in the spiritual lives of both lay and ordained people. He believed that monasteries could lead the way for the entire Church, and he was harshest in his criticism of monks themselves. To his mind, it was clear that when monks and lay ascetics reformed their ways and became more serious of purpose, and made public expressions of piety, more and more people would feel called to take up the mantle of a religious.

Damian was a firm believer that every monk must practice contemplation, and he had a great influence on the development of eremitic communities throughout Western Europe. He practiced severe forms of asceticism, including self-flagellation (which he called "apostolic scourging" in his letters) as well as long fasts. This kind of activity was uncommon among most clergy, who more often preferred subtler means of getting close to God such as study, quiet retreat, liturgy, and worship. Damian became notorious for challenging the authority of the clergy, particularly wayward bishops and priests, who were all too common. He was even known to curse at them. The practice of the "saintly curse"—using words like magic to pronounce divine judgment upon someone—is part of the color of medieval religious life.[1] In Ireland there was an old Druidic practice called "cursing from a height," in which one would go to an outcrop of land or an overlooking tower and shout maledictions down upon someone passing by, allowing the words to fall with great weight upon the intended recipient. As Christianity took hold and the pagan customs morphed into Christian spiritual practices, we see Irish religious, including Saint Ruadán, founder of a monastery at Tipperary, in occasional cursing contests with Druid priests. Similar traditions existed in medieval Italy, and Peter Damian would have appreciated this, for like the Old Testament prophets he had plenty to say about those whom he viewed as God's enemies in his own place and time.

In one of his letters, without explicitly calling down a curse, Damian addresses the monks of the famous monastery of Monte Cassino, eighty miles south of Rome, telling them that a certain cardinal who forbade the practice of flagellation in public had died suddenly precisely because of his ignorance. Damian advocated "apostolic scourging" every Friday as a way of participating in and commemorating the passion of Christ, who was flogged at the command of Pilate on the first Good Friday. Damian wrote in that letter to the Monte Cassino monks: "I shall make bold to say, my dear brothers, that anyone who is ashamed to remove his clothes that he might suffer with Christ, has undoubtedly listened to the word of the serpent."[2]

Toward the end of his life Damian wrote a passionate letter to the abbot of a Benedictine monastery. Damian had been accused of violating the Rule of Saint Benedict by accepting monks who had left another Benedictine community. In responding to the charge, Damian argues that the Rule and Benedictine life are more generally for novices, while a serious life of contemplation, even if outside one's home monastery, is what Benedict intended for the more mature monk. He writes:

Venerable abbot,

[Y]ou are angry with me, and complain that I am
accepting your monks into the hermitage contrary to
the precepts of our holy father, St. Benedict. . . . In
fact, [Benedict] even sanctions a brother after long
probation in a monastery, to learn how to fight in a
hermitage. . . . There he was a raw recruit, but here
he is a knight. . . . There he was a man coming from
the world, like one entering the small town of Zoar
after leaving Sodom; but when he passed over to the
hermitage, with Lot he now went up into the hill
country.[3]

In this letter, which would have been known to many
abbots and monks in Italy by the time Peter Angelerio
was at Faifula, Damian says: "Therefore, for one wishing
to reach the heights of perfection, the monastery must
be transitional, and not a place to stay; not a home, but a
hostel; not the destination we intend to reach, but a quiet
stop along the way."[4] According to Damian, there was a
greater religious ideal beyond that of a monk living in a
community.

Seeking God in Solitude

Peter Damian's militant ideas on what constituted a valuable spiritual life influenced many would-be monks and
hermits to follow him. For two centuries some of the most
dynamic Benedictine monks in Western Europe lived for
long periods of time as hermits, or left their monastic
houses in order to found new orders. Among them were

Abbot Robert of Molesme (ca. 1028–1111), who left the cloister more than once to live as a hermit and to lead groups of hermits before founding the famous abbey of Citeaux, south of Dijon, in 1098; Saint Stephen of Muret (1045–1124), who founded the abbey and order of Grandmont in his native France, after returning from Calabria, Italy, impressed with the vigor of the hermits there (Stephen produced no rule for the men of his order, calling true eremites apostles of Christ without need for anything but the Gospels);[5] Robert of Arbrissel (ca. 1060–1115), who led a group of hermits until his group, too, joined up with the Cistercians; and the Cistercian Norbert of Xanten (ca. 1080–1134), who became a hermit before he found the site where Saint Ursula's relics were hidden, and then founded the Premonstratensian order.

Under such influences, at twenty years of age Brother Peter felt drawn away from the monastery at Faifula, having grown dissatisfied with community life. This change may have been occasioned by the death of his mother, for it was sometime soon after his mother's death that Peter left the monastery. But more than that, the twenty-year-old Peter left seeking his own future as a solitary. From the Autobiography one gets the feeling that he is seeking to discover a bit of the world, because he wouldn't have seen much of anything up until that point. We see him wandering the mountains of the rugged Abruzzi in search of a place to stake his claim.

By about 1231, when he was twenty-one, Peter had taken up residence on the southernmost peak of the Maiella range, Mount Porrara.[6] He seems to have remained there for two years. Then eventually he made his way to Rome, in 1233 or 1234, where he was ordained a priest. It was during his year in Rome that Peter came to see the arrogance and misplaced ambitions of some of the clergy, their churches, and even the papacy, confirming in him the stringent ideals that he'd begun to practice since discovering the writings of Peter Damian and leaving the monastery.

But corruption can be found in all places, and along his journeys Peter met at least one disreputable solitary. Not all monks were holy men, Peter would find out. According to the story in the Autobiography, when Peter was leaving Rome to return to the mountains of Abruzzo he stopped to see a solitary, but God revealed to Peter "the man's dishonest life"—in order, it says, to keep Peter "from telling his secrets" to him. We do not learn the solitary's name or the nature of his sins; we know only that Peter had a God-given gift of discerning what was suspect. This man was not to be trusted.[7]

Our would-be hermit moved on. As he went in search of a new and more permanent residence in Abruzzo, the descriptions in his Autobiography are similar to the chronicles one might read of a long-distance hiker taking to the woods each morning with a pack on his back. On one occasion, Peter carries two loaves and some fish with him for the day (the symbolism is surely deliberate), and as he approaches the spot that he would later make his home, two beautiful women appear. Strange women is a familiar motif in the hagiographical lives of medieval saints. As in the much earlier Life of Saint Anthony of Egypt, in Peter's story women are despised as little more than temptresses, constantly snuggling up to him, naked, while he sleeps, and beckoning him to come in to be with them when he would rather be praying. In those days, religious men most often had one of two reactions to women: fear or resentment. Women were feared because of their differences, sometimes in ways that even seem comical. Even their handiwork became a subject of fear, as in this observation from a penitential text from about the year 1010:

> Have you been present when women have practiced their woolen work, in their webs, when they begin their webs hoping to be able to bring them about with incantations and when the threads of the warp and the woof become so mingled together that unless they supplement them with other incantations of the devil, the whole thing will collapse? If you have been present or consented to this, you shall do penance for thirty days on bread and water.

In such cases the fear went to even greater, more unreasonable, extremes, as in this passage from the same penitential text:

> Have you believed that there is any woman who can do what some have affirmed they do at the devil's command; that is, with a throng of demons transformed into the likenesses of women, ride on beasts on special nights and are numbered with their company? If you have participated in this infidelity, you should do penance for one year on the appointed fast days.[8]

Believing in these mythical powers of women to seduce was, in itself, a grave sin. In Peter's experience, two women are said to have "grappled with him, grabbing him with their hands." Later in a cave on another mountain he encounters other women in his dreams—demons in the form of women, the text says—and they tempt him, including "forcibly" trying to remove his tunic. It's impossible to read such accounts in the twenty-first century without seeing a subtext of wish fulfillment in addition to fear. Some might observe that these hagiographical stories demonstrate a male struggle with the shadowy feminine side of the subconscious. These internal conflicts are much less about sex and more about doubt. Such trials were said to have occurred before Peter ever made his permanent home on a holy mountain.

As was mentioned at the outset, it remains unclear how far Peter's Autobiography ought to be trusted as history. It isn't the purpose of this book to demonstrate the factuality of that text. But if we compare Peter's Autobiography to the hagiographical texts, it would appear that the latter are based on Peter's written experience, whether his Autobiography or other pieces of writing. How could it be otherwise, given that what is recorded next is a nocturnal emission: Peter admits to having had one. The story is told in the third person, which is understandable. And Peter worries over whether or not to celebrate Holy Communion the next morning, given that he had been sullied during the night. Surely no one but Peter could have had access to such information, and why would he reveal something of this sort unless he had pious reasons for wanting to share his own experiences?

Peter Sits Down to Fame

The Autobiography culminates when its subject is only thirty years old. After his return from Rome, and his wanderings back into the Abruzzi in search of a mountain retreat, Peter ultimately finds his way to the peak where he would make the hermitage that would make his name: Mount Morrone (6,700 feet), high in the Apennines. This is the place that would forever be marked by his presence, becoming his gate to heaven. It was sometime around 1235 when the anonymous monk made his rough and solitary home on a cliff. He who began adulthood as one of many in a cowl has become a hermit, abandoning world and monastery in order to seek his salvation. The text includes this fascinating, almost haiku-like, two-sentence description of what happened upon his first finding the cave upon Mount Morrone:

> *After entering, he sat down.*
> *A great snake appeared*
> *and then left.*

Peter would remain in his hermitage for ten years.

Others Follow

What happened next must have been surprising even—or especially—to Peter. Throughout the centuries, the spiritually enigmatic have easily gained followers. From the Buddha to John the Baptist to Saint Anthony of Egypt, lone, vigorous, earnest spiritual practitioners have drawn disciples from the cities and countryside, people seeking to deepen their spiritual experiences and radicalize their commitments to the ideals of their religious tradition. Within a short period of time, Peter was sought after as a spiritual director and a wise man, like the Desert Fathers (the models of the wise hermit that predated Peter by nearly a thousand years).

The rule of life that Peter followed when he organized a community of brother hermits was derived mostly from Saint Benedict, combined with tenets based on Peter's enthusiasm for Damian's reforming tendencies as well as Peter's own experiences of ascetic discipline and penitential practices. Peter was increasingly uninterested in the more cultivated ways of the large monastic orders, their easier ways of living. So he instituted such severities as saying the first office of Matins at 2 A.M., observing multiple "Lents" each year, and fasting on far more days than is required by the traditional Benedictine Rule. Such practices only served to gain him more followers.

"Word of mouth" truly meant something in those days, before the existence of social media and at about the time that mail was first being delivered. One person at a time would descend Mount Morrone having found something intangible that he'd been searching for, and upon returning to his place and ways of living would tell others about what he had experienced. People began flocking to find Peter, to ask for answers to questions about how they should live their lives, and about how things should be in the Church and the world. His teachings were memorable, his insight, penetrating. He seems to have known a man's sins before he even confessed them. Peter's commitment to the eremitic life had an authenticity that wasn't common among other hermits (for there were plenty in the mountains all over Europe) at that time. A Victorian-era commentator put it this way: "Others joined him. One by one they came to build their poor cells near him, their elder brother in spirit, their shining example in the contempt for earthly prizes."[9] Some of these men then stayed, and a new eremitical brotherhood was formed in the Benedictine spirit.

Peter would cite 1244 as the year when his order was founded, taking its inspiration from the life and writings of Peter Damian (who had been called a saint in Italy since his death in 1072). The members of Peter's community took to calling themselves the Hermits of Saint Damian, but also, unceremoniously, they were sometimes simply known as Morronites, after the mountain where they lived. They wouldn't have a Rule for another ten years, so 1254 is also given as the year of their founding. They received papal confirmation, from Urban IV, on June 1, 1263. Finally, precisely half a century after the first men gathered around Peter on the mountain, their name would change in honor of their founder's change of status. They would become known as the Celestines.

The spirituality of Peter's community soon became more Camaldolese than Benedictine—focusing more on solitary study and prayer than on praying and working in a community—during these early eremitic days. Peter was inspired by the ideals of the earlier Italian hermit Saint Romuald (ca. 950–1025), the founder of the Camaldolese order; the first biography of Romuald was written by Peter's hero, Peter Damian. Romuald was a strict reformer of monasteries and monasticism, so strict, in fact, that his monks rebelled against his methods, hurrying Romuald toward the hermit life. He went on to become a leader of the "Renaissance of eremitical asceticism" that had occurred two centuries before Peter Morrone came on the scene.[10]

When Damian praised Romuald, it was often for his ability to put the fear of God into the hearts of secular rulers. Damian wrote:

When Rainerius had become lord of the region
[the Margrave of Tuscany], he used to say that,
"Not the Emperor, not any other man, is able to
strike great fear into me in the way that the appearance of Romuald terrifies me—before his face I do
not know what to say, nor can I find any excuses
by which I could defend myself." In truth, the holy
man possessed by divine gift the grace that whatever sinners, especially powerful men of the world,
would come into his presence would soon be struck
with internal trembling as if they were in the presence of the majesty of God.[11]

Such accounts served as inspiration to any man who was
attracted to the power that comes with religious authority.
At times, Romuald's sayings (made popular in a brief Rule
that he is alleged to have written), sound Zen-like in their
simplicity. Among them are the following:

Sit in your cell as if you are in paradise.

Leave the entire world behind you. Forget it.

Empty yourself completely and wait patiently, con-
tent with God.

Be like the chick who eats nothing but what his
mother brings to him.

These things Peter did gladly.
By 1244 or 1245, when he was thirty-four or thirty-five,
Peter needed to escape those who were coming to seek
his advice and counsel, so he fled to the heights of the
limestone peak of Mount Maiella (9,100 feet), a place

that would become renowned because he lived there. Maiella is the tallest mountain in the area, tucked away on the less accessible northern end of the range. There Peter established a more remote hermitage, near today's town of Roccamorice in the province of Pescara. In leaving for Maiella, Peter seems to have been motivated by the need for what we today sometimes call "visual privacy," a need to be shielded from the eyes of one's neighbors; the Autobiography refers to the deforestation of Mount Morrone as a motivating factor of his decision to move.

Although a new order of hermits would soon begin, Peter's companions didn't exactly accompany him to the new heights immediately. The Autobiography says that he went alone at first, which may indicate Peter's propensity for independent, even stubborn, decision making. He didn't consult with his brothers before going. Eventually (the hagiography says, within "a few days"), they were convinced to join him, seeing that he wouldn't change his mind.

A generation later, Petrarch would refer to Maiella as *Domus Christi,* or the "House of Christ," because of the number of hermitages and monasteries, caves and rock churches, there.[12] His residence on this higher and more difficult mountain became for Peter a symbol of his increasing desire to leave the world completely behind. Maiella has always been known as a difficult place to visit, and an even more challenging place to leave. To this day, the word *Maiella* is shorthand in the Abruzzi for an omen or a curse. An Italian writer and political revolutionary of the last century describes it as follows: "Here, where countless hermits once lived, in more recent times hundreds of outlaws have hidden, or escaped prisoners of war, or partisans, many of them helped by the local people."[13]

Mountains are holy in nearly every place and faith. In

Italy (as in Ireland, Greece, India, Japan) they have always been pilgrimage destinations. In the late Middle Ages there were European legends of a "paradise of delights" in the Far East—somewhere near the confluence of the Tigris and Euphrates Rivers—a place where contemplatives might live a life more like that of the angels. Peter dreamed of such a place. But there is also a word of Latin derivation, *ultramontane,* which means "those who live beyond the mountains," and this gets at what Peter desired, as well. The word was usually applied to non-Italian popes who were quite literally from lands beyond the Alps. But there is a deeper meaning, too. A man who is ultramontane is an outsider, and this was a position that Peter settled into comfortably. He would occasionally travel to Rome, or elsewhere in Molise and Abruzzo, establishing new associations of monks and hermits, but for decades his greatest wish was to be the one who stands on the outside looking in.

9

THE HUNDRED-METER FAST

The tops of the Maiella mountains are remote and uninviting. En route to the highest peaks at 9,000 feet, wild boar feed on pungent herbs. A few dozen Marsican brown bear still roam freely, and one sees the occasional peregrine falcon. Some of the Maiella's caves are half a mile long, all underground. Peter explored many of them. "The Lord showed me a large cave that pleased me very much," he writes in his Autobiography. "Only one of my monks wanted to join me at first, but eventually more came," he says.

His early followers complained about the height, the distance, and the arduousness of life on Maiella. "We are exhausted and can hardly even make it up here," they told him. One night in the high heat of June, when the top of the mountain hadn't seen rain for weeks, all of the brother monks were gathered around Peter's cave, listening to him preach when suddenly they witnessed a fire break out and spread rapidly to a pile of dry branches. Monks had been using branches to create their own makeshift huts near Peter's cave until more suitable dwellings could be arranged. The branches had dried as effectively as if they were intended for kindling, and they lit up like candles in the early evening hour. Peter's entire cell appeared to be aflame.

"Get up . . . *Now!*" Peter yelled to them. "Throw every branch out of here!"

With quick hands, the monks picked up the burning faggots and tossed them away from the greenery, in the direction of the rocks. They separated what was smoldering from what was as yet untouched by the heat and flames. And within a few minutes the threat had abated. Moments later, raising his hands to heaven, Peter began to thank God for his goodness and protection. But some of the brothers were slow to follow.

"Why did you ever come to this place?" one muttered, kicking at some of the remaining glowing embers. His comment was echoed by one brother after another. Peter looked at them all and said, "My whole body could burn, and yet I wouldn't leave this place."

There has always been a connection in the mystical and ascetical strands of Christianity between mountains and contemplation. As one leaves the world behind, literally ascending higher and higher in elevation away from city and civilization, one also climbs a metaphorical mountain of contemplation. Self-imposed exile offered the religious man an opportunity to cast a critical eye on civilization below. To be in the mountains was to have moved beyond the desert. These two climatic metaphors engrossed a hermit's imagination. The desert was the place

for purgation: repentance, cleansing, attempting to remove the stain of earthly life and its carnal hold on the
human soul. The mountain was beyond this. It was quite
literally an ascent, a place for holiness. "Who shall ascend
the hill of the Lord? And who shall stand in his holy place?"
the psalmist writes (Ps. 24:3). Peter Maiella (aka Morrone)
joined the august tradition of those, like Moses, who met
the Lord face-to-face on Mount Sinai. Such a life wasn't for
everyone.

The life of a hermit was only for the hearty and healthy.
Like a worthy competitor, Saint Romuald was praised by
Peter Damian for the extreme severity of his penances.
Norbert of Xanten, a contemporary of Romuald's and a
cofounder of the eleventh-century eremitic renaissance,
also became a saint by demonstrating the power of his
mind to discipline his body. One thing Norbert did to
prove the point was to walk everywhere barefoot and wearing only animal skins.

Some of the great athletes of their day, hermits had to
be able to endure excruciating silence, food that didn't
nourish or satisfy, an almost complete lack of physical contact with others, arduous work, uncomfortable sleeping
conditions, a general lack of sleep, and extremes of cold
and heat. These were the natural conditions they faced
before they imposed any hardships on themselves.

For Peter and his brothers, in order to be worth-
while the spiritual life had to be difficult. Having a relationship with God was expected to be tough, and it could
only begin when one had completely surrendered one's
life to divine pursuits. The hard existence of the hermit had one other benefit as well. It offered a way of
sanctifying what might have otherwise been a miserable

existence. A hermit, like anyone with a very close relationship with God, takes his suffering into his own hands, turning to holy purposes the difficulties of everyday life.

The hermits would encourage one another by reading from Palladius of Galatia's accounts of the lives of the Desert Fathers. His classic *Lausiac History* was "like a wonderbook, to show what these spiritual athletes could take upon themselves for the love of Christ. In the presence of the assembled community the stories of these mortified lives were read aloud. Inevitably, for souls so avid for perfection, they became so many incitements to heroism."[1] Peter knew well the life of one of these, an ascetic named Saint Simeon Stylites (ca. 390–459), whose feast was celebrated each year on January 5. This Syrian shepherd became a monk as a teenager and quickly desired to become a spiritual standout, finding unusual ways to demonstrate his prowess. He would remain standing for days at a time and abstain from food for even longer periods. People followed him and then imitated him. They became almost like the bodybuilders of the 1970s, exhibiting themselves in front of large crowds at public beaches in California or Florida. In similar ways, people came to witness the wondrous ways that Simeon challenged his body. Simeon was so determined to stand apart from the other ascetics of the desert that he ascended a pillar and remained there for more than three decades. His first pillar was about twelve feet tall, and by the end of his life he stood upon one that was forty-five feet high. Before long, there were several men living atop pillars near Simeon. They took a name for themselves—stylites—which comes from the Greek, meaning "pillar saints." The famous agnostic/cynic Edward

Gibbon had a rare admiration for this bizarre religious man. He wrote in *History of the Decline and Fall of the Roman Empire:*

> In this last and lofty station, the Syrian Anachoret resisted the heat of thirty summers, and the cold of as many winters. Habit and exercise instructed him to maintain his dangerous situation without fear or giddiness, and successively to assume the different postures of devotion. He sometimes prayed in an erect attitude, with his outstretched arms in the figure of a cross, but his most familiar practice was that of bending his meager skeleton from the forehead to the feet; and a curious spectator, after numbering twelve hundred and forty-four repetitions, at length desisted from the endless account.

But there is a note of sorrow in many of the stories of great ascetics from the past. Simeon seems to have felt that he could escape the world vertically—that perhaps if he went high enough, if he denied himself enough, God would take him to heaven, like Elijah on a chariot. Simeon died all alone up on his perch.

Did our hermit wish for something similar?

As a physical specimen, Peter would have been well built, with solid legs, knees hardened from decades of kneeling, and feet so calloused that he could step on a bumblebee without being disturbed by its sting. The face of Peter-cum-Celestine V as it appears atop his tomb in L'Aquila still today is a lean, gaunt visage with high cheekbones, deeply set eyes, and a soft chin. There is a determination about his pursed lips that cannot be accidental.

Another image of Peter, drawn three centuries later, shows that same face with a beard, a head that is mostly bald but flowing with hair on both sides. This drawing, too, is from an anonymous hand, and is titled simply *Fr. Petrus Confessor.*[2]

For several months a year, the nights and early mornings were raw and frigid and unforgiving on mounts Morrone and Maiella. Peter loved these small hardships. He and many of his brother hermits reveled in the type of inconveniences and difficulties that the wealthier in Rome, Paris, and Naples sought to avoid. At times in the Autobiography, we see Peter reminding the others of their commitment to these hardships as an expression of true love for God. A Hermit of Saint Damian was just the sort who might get a pebble caught in his sandal first thing in the morning, and then leave it lodged there for the rest of the day believing that the pain might teach him something profound about carrying the cross of Christ.

The difficulties of the natural environment were not enough for these men. They believed that obeying Christ meant suffering as he had. They took seriously Christ's words to his disciples: "For whoever would save his life will lose it; and whoever loses his life for my sake, he will save it" (Lk. 9:24). For them the promise of salvation and eternal life in heaven—a promise made to those who suffered on earth—took precedence over considerations of comfort in this life. And so, being human, these hermits competed with one another. And having left the world behind, there wasn't much to compete about except spiritual matters.

Often the spiritual became physical. One man would pray alone in his cell from the time of morning prayer until evening, and would do so while standing. Another man would hear of this and then commit to stand in prayer all through the night until daybreak. And so on.

Peter took to wearing a hair shirt like John the Baptist and Francis of Assisi. Hair shirts were made of the roughest animal hair, usually goat hair, roughened with knots to ensure that the person wearing it would be in constant discomfort. The practice goes back to the Hebrew Bible's reference to putting on sackcloth and ashes in prayer and supplication to God. "Sackcloth" was probably the equivalent of an early hair shirt (Dn. 9:3. See also Ps. 35:13).

Peter also fasted regularly, including the sort of fasting that was once popular with living saints: observing multiple "Lents" throughout the year. The discipline of the Great Lent (as it is called in the East), the forty weekdays leading up to Easter, was practiced at other times of the year. Special fasts would be kept, together with rigorous devotion to prayer and perhaps penitential physical labor. A famous example of a mystical experience that followed upon such a period of Lenten observances is part of the legend of Francis of Assisi. It was September 1224, and Francis had come to Mount Alverno in the Apennines with a few of his closest companions intending to pray for forty days, until the Feast of Saint Michael. During that time Francis encountered Christ in the form of a six-winged angel, and then he received the stigmata. That first recorded instance of the stigmata provided inspiration that mystics needed to fast.

Some hermits would go further in their own, personal practice. Fasting for weeks on end became common. Some bragged about taking the Host as their only sustenance. Just as the ancient Greek athletes would astonish crowds with their feats of endurance and strength, Christian ascetics such as Peter Maiella were the true athletes of the later Middle Ages.

We know from the Autobiography that while Peter and his brother hermits occupied themselves, as any good religious would, in the daily practice of praying the Liturgy of the Hours, Peter struggled with snow, dreams, and demons atop Mount Maiella. The group built an oratory, which is not a full parish church but a place for more simple prayer and celebrating the Mass—where they would gather to sing the office. The building was situated only ten paces from Peter's cave. They would often pray at the same time but separately, in their own cells and caves, and occasionally they would come together in the oratory. It became a place of great mystery. It has been recorded that unknown voices were heard singing the late-night prayers in the oratory, and when a brother went in to look, there was no one there.

They also had to contend with evil spirits. At one point Peter tells of "some of the brothers"—it sounds like he's speaking of himself—"spying throngs of demons in the forest."

"They were bleating like sheep, wanting to get into the oratory," Peter says. It is easy to imagine the fear that might grip the heart of a sensitive man, attuned to divine messages, on top of a mountain in the middle of the night.

Among the signs and wonders Peter recorded is a story of a dove alighting time and again in the midst of the hermits, refusing to leave this special place of prayer. It was soon decided that this was a sign that the Holy Spirit had claimed the spot. This is the legend of how the hermit settled upon the name Santo Spirito, or "Holy Spirit," for the monastery near Sulmona that would become his order's motherhouse. It was also a name fitting Peter's belief that he was living in the third and final epoch of the history of the world, one guided and governed by the third member of the Trinity.[3]

Above all, Peter relished the remoteness of this place. One scholar calls him a "relatively mute, miracle-bearing, eremitic, mountain saint."[4] Maybe that was so. In the way that saints are made in Catholic tradition and legend, it was this geographical feature—Peter's difficult mountains— that made the man. He was not only formed by his place, but the narrative of his life and faith, as it was told and re- told in the centuries after he lived, makes sense only when we see it set in this craggy geography. While he sat with the doves on his massif, challenging his body to suffer for his God, he began to desire to grow the movement that he had started.

WALKING TO LYON

For the next twenty years, Peter Morrone, now also known as Peter Maiella, slowly and deliberately built his brotherhood from a handful of hermits into dozens of communities with oratories all over central Italy. Beginning in 1244 or 1245, when he was thirty-four or thirty-five years old, until 1264 he blended a life of retreat from civilization with enough entrées into the world of influence to garner favors of land, stone, supplies, and protection for his growing order. We know almost nothing about Peter's day-to-day existence when he was in his thirties and forties, except that the Hermits of Saint Damian continued to grow.

By 1264, when Peter was fifty-five, the bishop of Chieti was approached to approve the first rule of life for the hermits. Northeast of Rome, Chieti is a capital city as well as a province, which is part of Abruzzo. The city lies only one mile from the shores of the Adriatic, the Maiella mountains standing proudly on the other side. This bishop of Chieti, Niccolò of Fossa, was a cousin of Pope Innocent III and a nephew of Pope Gregory IX. He has gone down in history as a prime example of nepotism run amok in the medieval Italian Church. Nevertheless, he clearly knew Peter Maiella and admired his way of life.[1] Once Niccolò put his stamp of approval on the Rule it was then sent to Pope Urban IV in Rome, who added his own approval as one of his last acts. Urban would die in Perugia on October 2, 1264.

Peter's ambition was fully evident during this time. Had it not been, we would know almost nothing of him from history. There were hundreds of anonymous hermits living in the Apennines during the two generations that Peter's life spanned. There had been hundreds before them dating back all the way to late antiquity. Few of these men founded new religious orders. Fewer still lobbied popes and cardinals for favors so that those orders might grow.

By the end of the 1260s, Peter was feeling the need for formal, papal approval for his order. Despite their early successes and support, the Hermits of Saint Damian were, like many fledgling monastic orders, operating outside of the jurisdiction of the Church. They were unprotected. Their privilege to exist, their approved status as an organ of the Church, and most tangibly their houses, churches, and other property could be revoked without notice unless they came under the oversight and protection of a cardinal or another ruler approved by Rome. Peter knew that he needed final, definitive protection and he began to ponder how to accomplish this.

On August 25, 1270, Charles I's older brother, Louis IX, King of France, died (soon after he would be made a saint). The Eighth Crusade had been launched by Louis just months earlier, and Louis himself had led the crusaders toward Syria, attempting to free Christian outposts in Syria that had fallen into Muslim hands. They made it only

as far as Tunis and there the elderly Louis, the most renowned and respected man in the world at the time, died.
By October 30 of that year, the crusader positions in Tunis
were abandoned as part of a truce with the sultan of Egypt.
The crusading era seemed to be finally over, and the
focus of both secular and religious leaders turned toward
strengthening rule and relationships at home.

From almost the moment that he took office in 1271,
Pope Gregory X (1271–76) announced his intention to
convene the fourteenth ecumenical council of the Roman
Catholic Church in Lyon, in east-central France. All of
the world's key leaders would gather at what came to be
known as the Second Council of Lyon. Peter knew that
there a man might gain access to every powerful person of
ecclesiastical importance alive.

It was on a midwinter day of 1273–74 that the sixty-
four-year-old Peter gathered a few of his friends and a
handful of belongings for the walk to Lyon, located mid-
way between Paris and Marseilles. They strapped on their
sandals, picked up their staffs, slipped their breviaries
into their tunic pockets, and began their slow descent.
They were hoping to reach their destination during the
summer when the holy father, his cardinals, representatives of the kingdoms of Germany, France, England, Sicily, Norway, Hungary, Bohemia, and hundreds of bishops
and prelates from all over Europe would be assembled. A
journey of approximately seven hundred miles, or eleven
or twelve hours by automobile today, in Peter's day would
have taken three or four months. Their route would have
taken them through Bologna and Turin, from monastery
to monastery, oratory to oratory, many of them among the
dozens in their own order, and they would stop each night
at another house along the way.

Pope Gregory X had selected Lyon as the location for this fourteenth ecumenical council because it had been the site of the thirteenth, but also because it was clearly outside the territory of Charles I of Anjou, whose motivations he never trusted.[2]

The pope's intention was nothing less than to reunite the two branches of the Christian Church: East and West. To that end, Gregory X invited emissaries of the Byzantine emperor Michael VIII in an effort to repair rifts that had occurred between the two branches of Christendom two centuries earlier, during what was known as the Great Schism. Emperor Michael had just retaken Constantinople from the hands of Western princes, whom he then kindly asked to maintain their own kingdoms and leave the Eastern Church alone. Gregory reached out to him for reasons of his own, and Michael agreed to send his ambassadors to Lyon.

Before the distinguished visitors and guests arrived to meet Gregory X, hanging like a pall over the Second Council of Lyon was the death of the Western Church's greatest theologian, Thomas Aquinas. Summoned by the pope to attend the Council, Aquinas died en route on March 7, 1274, after sustaining a wound to his head after striking it on a tree. There were those who suspected Charles I of playing a sinister role in murdering the great theologian since one of Aquinas's many teachings was that an illegitimate king could rightfully be overthrown by the people or the pope, even by means of regicide, if it was God's pleasure. This was a controversial idea particularly in the era of the "divine right of kings," and certainly Charles took note of such insolence. But he didn't kill Aquinas. Those theories have long ago been discounted.

The other great thinker to die in connection with the

Council was the Franciscan Bonaventure, who came to his end during the Council's final week, on July 15, 1274, while he was attending the sessions. And as we mentioned in chapter two, he was poisoned.

There were other spectacles in Lyon. The gathering was the stuff of great theater. Men gathered from all over the known world, as far east as Iran and as far west as Ireland, with attendants donning various types of ceremonial dress. There were cardinals and bishops, princes and mercenaries. The Persian Il-khanate, part of the Mongol Empire, sent a delegation, because his people were hoping to enlist the aid of their Christian counterparts to fight their common enemy the Muslim Mamluks. While in Lyon, the leader of the Il-Khans, Abaqa Khan (1234–82), appears to have instructed some of his delegation to undergo Christian baptism, as a goodwill gesture, much to the shock of those present. The ceremony was conducted by none other than the bishop of Ostia, the future Pope Innocent V.

Abaqa Khan was renowned for working closely with Christians throughout his rule, usually in efforts to defeat Muslims, but also in genuine attempts to form peaceful alliances of other kinds. He had no designs upon Christian lands in the West; his only aim was to maintain his own kingdom's footing in the East. But it remains a mystery as to why he went to the extent of having some among his party baptized. No doubt he did not understand that for Christians new life and responsibilities underlie the ritual. The assent to be baptized, interpreted as conversions by people like Gregory X and Edward I of England, must have had a more confused legacy in the Persian East, as many of the coins and emblems of the Mongol's rule—still seen in museums around the world today—display Christian symbols, including "In the name of the Father, the Son, and the Holy Spirit."

Between May 7 and July 17, delegates gathered around Pope Gregory X to discuss issues of worldwide ecclesiastical importance. Hundreds of bishops listened and occasionally debated the viability of uniting the churches, securing lost outposts such as Acre, and keeping the Muslims at bay. A variety of measures were on the table, and constitutions were written on such topics as financing new Crusades through taxation, the importance of excommunicating pirates who acted outside of recognized boundaries of behavior during Crusades, and the plenary indulgence granted to any man willing to join a holy campaign. A resolution was passed saying the Church must henceforth take more seriously the decision made earlier in the century to prohibit the founding of new religious orders. Abaqa Khan left the Council with a resolution declaring that the Western Church would coordinate with the Il-Khans before launching any more campaigns against their mutual enemies upon the eastern border of their kingdoms in Syria and Egypt.[3] Such cooperation would never materialize, however, because the crusading spirit had ebbed out of the papacy and the princes, including Charles I; they were more interested in securing the lands of Western European Christendom than in risking further losses in the Holy Land.

Also at the Council of Lyon, Pope Gregory X was able to secure agreement from Emperor Michael VIII for a full reunification of the Eastern Church with the West, including an acquiescence regarding Rome's primacy. But when Michael VIII returned home to his empire, there was insufficient backing from among the clergy and bishops of the Greek churches for any further action to be taken on such an agreement. And for his part in participating in this attempt to unify the churches, even today Michael VIII Palaeologus is referred to as a traitor by many Eastern Christians.

At Lyon Gregory X also instituted his new instructions on the election of future popes in conclave. As we saw in chapter two, it was at the ecumenical council of 1274 that the rules for conclaves were laid out in detail (only to be rescinded by Gregory's successors). All of these resolutions were made into ecclesiastical law by papal decree on November 1.

For his part, Peter ended up arriving late. He had walked to Lyon in order to plead for the continued ecclesiastical independence and protection of his still relatively new brotherhood. But by the time he arrived many of the delegates had already left and all were mourning the death of Aquinas. A solemnity hung over the streets from the weight of business being conducted.

Still, Peter found his way to representatives of Pope Gregory X and achieved his goal: his brotherhood of hermits would be formally incorporated as a branch of the Benedictine order. A new order would not be created, as the Council had just admonished themselves for permitting too many new orders to be founded over the previous century. The Hermits of Saint Damian would remain under the Benedictine umbrella. But even more important to Peter, at the suggestion of Pope Gregory, the monasteries would be protected by Charles I of Anjou, who already controlled all of the territory surrounding the order's many oratories. Peter was jubilant. A victory had been won.

Settling Down for Good

As he and his brothers made their way back to the Abruzzi, they traveled through the Mediterranean port city of Genoa, where they may have visited with Jacobus Voragine, the archbishop, who was at that moment finishing his compilation of the lives of the saints that would come to be known as *The Golden Legend*. From Genoa they made their way south through Florence, the capital city of Tuscany, where the Italian florin, the gold coin that became Europe's standard currency, had originated. There they probably sought support for their efforts in the form of money or supplies, as well as the donation of Tuscan property for the foundation of a new religious community for their order. From Florence they traveled down into the scattered and more remote and familiar hill towns of Umbria and then Abruzzo, eventually stopping for a night on a hill known as Collemaggio on the outskirts of L'Aquila, not far from Peter's childhood home.

Settling down for the night on this hillside, Peter fell asleep in his makeshift cell and began to dream. According to the story that he himself told late in life and that was repeated throughout his canonization hearings decades later, the Virgin Mary appeared to Peter surrounded by angels on stairs of gold, a vision reminiscent of the story of Jacob's Ladder in the book of Genesis. The Blessed Virgin asked Peter to build a church in her honor. He took note of this, but then the next morning, Peter rose early and he and his companions continued on their way back to Santo Spirito, another two days away. Finally, on Maiella,

Peter triumphantly convened the first general chapter of his order with all of his brethren present from the communities across Molise and Abruzzo, joyfully informing them all of Gregory X's blessing on their efforts. It was then that the Hermits of Saint Damian formally reiterated that the Rule of Saint Benedict was to be their rule of life.

But Peter didn't forget his dream at Collemaggio. In fact, he told others about it, and again, by the skills of fund-raising, organization, and persuasion that characterized the hermit's adult life, by 1283 he and his brothers had purchased the Collemaggio hill near L'Aquila and broken ground for a church to be dedicated to the Blessed Virgin. Five years later they consecrated the as yet unfinished structure Santa Maria of Collemaggio, the Basilica of Saint Mary.

This was a bittersweet time for Peter. Certainly, he had done the work of the Blessed Mother, but the basilica would also increase the popularity of the St. Damian Hermits. In turn, more pilgrims and tourists would flock to the man who after intense moments of activity and creativity only seemed to desire to be alone again with his God.[4]

His primary work was done, but Peter's reputation grew ever more rapidly. In 1276 the monastery at which he had entered religious life, Santa Maria of Faifula, convinced him to return as their part-time abbot. And three years later, he also took on the abbot's responsibilities of San Giovanni monastery in the diocese of Lucera, part of the Foggia province in southern Italy.

In the fifteen years after the Second Council of Lyon, from 1275 to 1290, his name was often heard in the corridors of power. The papal curia and the royal courts of Naples, Sicily, Paris, Avignon, and beyond knew of his fame as a mystic and leader of men. He was said to possess miraculous powers of healing. In 1280, at the age of seventy-one, Peter took a journey to Rome. There he was met with plaudits, came to know more men of influence, and was granted two more monasteries for his work of turning common men into angels. Throughout his sixties and seventies, this hermit who longed for intense periods of seclusion was one of the most peripatetic of holy men, visiting his growing collection of religious houses. By the time he was seventy-six, in 1285, he had acquired another already established monastery, San Pietro, in the Abruzzi near Manoppello.[5]

All during this time, Peter's renown hindered him from living the solitary religious life that he envisioned for himself and his brothers. He didn't seem to grasp how his desires for stability and security and his need for recognition and adulation from his religious colleagues conflicted with his otherwise spiritual, sometimes very personal, religious intentions. It seemed that whenever he accomplished something great before the eyes of others, he soon felt the need to retreat from sight. Perhaps he wanted to model his life on the life of Jesus, who spent his public life healing and teaching, only to retreat into the desert, push out into the sea, or settle himself in a secluded garden or a mountaintop, to pray for a while.

After serving as abbot for several abbeys for decades, by 1293, when he was eighty-three, Peter was weary of the attention and the responsibility of governing communities of monks, and he moved away from sight once more. The essentially restless eremite returned to his previous home, to the now more quiet environs of Mount Morrone. Grateful to be back where he'd spent the first years of his solitary vocation, he settled into a regular life of solitude, begging to simply be left alone.

On Mount Morrone Peter found a small grotto where he could pursue his faith in quietude. It became a treasured place to him. Into the rocky face of the mountain he built a special oratory he named Eremo di Sant'Onofrio (the Hermitage of St. Onofrio).

Onofrio is Italian for the Latin name Onuphrius, a fifth-century hermit in Upper Egypt. He's a mythical figure, revered as a monk who left the monastery for the eremitic life and exemplified the solitary life with valor, courage, and tenacity. In iconography, Onofrio is usually depicted with long, wild hair and a loincloth made entirely of leaves. He looks like the original "wild man," and he was even called such in his own day, only to become the favorite saint of hermits a few centuries later.

Although Peter would ultimately spend only one year at Onofrio before the world again came calling, in the space of that year the place became recognized around the world for its piety. Like Moses on Sinai, Peter communed with the Almighty upon Morrone. For Peter, that year, 1293, was one of intense dedication to private, mental prayer. Begging to be left alone, once again a cave became Peter's room, and a rock, his pillow.

PART III
TURBULENT TIMES

Peter of Morrone . . . beware of the cheats,

Who'd have you think, that

Black is white and white is black as ink.

If in their snares you unguardedly sink,

You will sing your song most evilly.

—JACOPONE OF TODI
"Epistle to Pope Celestine V"

OBSESSED WITH SALVATION

The people of the Middle Ages were obsessed with salvation, with the fate of their souls and bodies after life on
earth was over. Perhaps this has been true of every people in every era everywhere, but it was especially true of
thirteenth-century men and women.

Wandering preachers would expound on a verse like
Ecclesiastes 12:7: "and the dust returns to the earth as it was,
and the spirit returns to God who gave it," while holding
up skulls for their crowd's inspection. *Look on this! For it will
very soon be you!* they would shout. The prospect of biologi-
cal death was terrifying—is terrifying, still—but imagine
the grip that it had on people who knew nothing of modern science. People of the Middle Ages relied on religion
alone to explain life and death. They had not yet entered
the period of Enlightenment when the traditions, texts,
and worldviews of religion could be either challenged or
counterbalanced with scientific understandings of germs,
viruses, and sanitation. Death was even more certain then
than it is now. After death, how could a person be sure that

her eternity would be heavenly? In those days, the answer was simple: only through the graces of the Church.

Then, as now, Christians confessed their sins to their priest and after confession, sought absolution and forgiveness. Usually a penance was imposed by the priest, often small deeds to be done or prayers to be said. Sometimes the priest would ask the penitent to make a pilgrimage, usually to a local shrine because most people at the time had little money and means for making longer journeys—although there were instances when a journey to Jerusalem would be recommended. A journey of that magnitude would heal a soul of nearly any sin that had been committed, simply because of the connection it would establish between the sinner and the earthly presence of Christ. Such a connection was more powerful to the medieval imagination than that of Christ in the Eucharist—because the average man or woman was rarely if ever permitted to receive Holy Communion. Concern for salvation and belief in the afterlife, including the trials of purgatory—where souls go to be made ready for heaven—were so intense that seeking indulgences (remission of punishment for sins) measured in days became common. At this time, indulgences were granted to Christians who paid money to the Church. For instance, one could earn a reprieve of one hundred days in purgatory for contributing a day's wages to the construction of a new church. Or two hundred days' escape from purgatory if you walked the Road to Santiago.

At the time of the First Crusade (1095), when Pope Urban II was whipping up audiences with fervor to join the cause, he was known to say: "Each man who joins in God's work to free the Holy Land will have his entire penance remitted!" This was one of the first instances of what came to be called an indulgence. The word carries a connotation today of a parent extending special grace and forgiveness to a child. So it was to the medieval sinner. But the indulgence granted by Urban II to the would-be crusader was atypical; it was a *plenary* indulgence—one that carried forgiveness for a lifetime's worth of venial (forgivable) sin. Join the Crusade and if you die during the holy cause your salvation is guaranteed, no stop in purgatory necessary, no matter what sins you may have previously committed. That was the promise. Such was the obsession with salvation that men would leave home and family and travel across the world to fight and likely die from wounds or starvation—because of the promise of eternal rest for their souls. Obviously, after this time the practice of granting indulgences for money went too far, and the Church, in time, came to acknowledge its own sin, admitting, "No institution, however holy, has entirely escaped abuse through the malice or unworthiness of man."[1]

But indulgences were popular while Peter was growing up. They were to be had at many of the great churches of Rome and elsewhere. The practice became so widespread by 1215 that the Church began putting limits on them. The Fourth Lateran Council limited the length of time to forty days maximum that could be offered by any bishop to one who observed the feast day of a patron saint. This decree doesn't seem to have been followed, however, as it was reissued time and again in the decades that followed.[2]

There was too much power in the hands of the Church in general and the pope in particular. Movements and reforms were at work—including vernacular translations of Scripture, the reformation of monastic orders, and the growth of lay movements such as the flagellants—that would slowly and naturally ease some of this power away from the hierarchy, putting greater spiritual responsibility into the hands of individual believers.

Salvation, broadly speaking, began to be offered in other aspects of life. During this century universities of higher learning were founded, opening up a new avenue for study and advancement that wasn't completely overseen by the Church. Young men had new career options, including studying to become physicians and surgeons and lawyers working in civil courts, just as earlier becoming a knight or a soldier was a choice for young men who wanted to serve the Church. As an example of the latter, Guibert of Nogent wrote: "God has instituted in our time holy wars, so that the order of knights and the crowd running in their wake . . . might find a new way of gaining salvation. And so they are not forced to abandon secular affairs completely by choosing the monastic life or any religious profession . . . but can attain in some measure God's grace while pursuing their own careers."[3] There were many ways to find freedom in this world and the next.

But most important of all were the spiritual groups that developed to satisfy the hungering for heaven that filled ordinary people. As churches focused more on their power and position, these groups focused on asceticism and reforming everyday life in light of spiritual ideals. They were ahead of their time and preceded the greatest mass spiritual movements of the era: those inaugurated by Saint Francis and Saint Dominic. There was an "evangelical awakening" going on at the turn of the thirteenth century as people throughout Western Europe sought more intense experiences of God and spiritual life for themselves.[4]

One such group was the Humiliati, who originated in Italy in the early twelfth century as an odd association of laypeople who dressed plainly and practiced asceticism (fasting, avoiding any form of comfort), devoting themselves to charity and good works. The name *Humiliati* refers to their desire to "humiliate" themselves publicly, which they did. They were easily identified in Italian towns because they refused to wear colorful clothing, opting for utter plainness. Saint Bernard of Clairvaux advised them for a time, and in 1134 at his urging many Humiliati men sought the permission of their wives to enter monasteries. It was sometimes disconcerting to local priests and bishops that a spiritual movement initiated by laypeople might be leading people in the ways of Spirit. But the Humiliatis' efforts were approved by Pope Innocent III in 1201, the same pope who befriended Francis of Assisi a decade later. By the late thirteenth century it was common for people in small villages throughout Italy to adopt Humiliati practices in addition to attending church services and devoting themselves to the usual roles of domestic life. Even today there are loose-knit groups of spiritually minded ascetics in remote parts of Italy who call themselves descendants of the medieval Humiliati.[5]

There were other movements, as well. Arnold of Brescia (d. 1155), an Italian monk who was active as a reformer of the Church through asceticism, became a vocal critic of papal political power. His superiors ordered Arnold to confine himself to a monastery, but he refused, managing to travel all over Italy preaching repentance and change. He was outspoken on the nobility of poverty as the key to a true, spiritual life. In his sermons, he insisted on what might seem obvious from our perspective today: that the holy father should provide mostly spiritual, rather than political, leadership. Eventually Arnold of Brescia was hanged for heresy by an early embodiment of the

Inquisition, after he questioned the value of the sacraments and the necessity for priests.

The Waldensians also arose as a reform movement during this era of spiritual and religious fermentation, although they traced their origins back to the fourth century when Constantine first institutionalized Christianity. They were spurred on by the teachings and example of Peter Waldo (d. 1218), a wealthy French clothier who underwent a dramatic conversion, leaving his property with his wife, giving his money to the poor, and taking to the road as a beggar. Waldo and those who followed him were often called "The Poor of Lyon" since Waldo was raised in that region. The Waldensians traveled all over France, Germany, and Italy urging people to seek a common, simple life, as opposed to a life centered on what we would today call middle-class priorities.

But chief among all of these wandering ascetics were the Cathars, a people who traced their identity back to the Gnostics of the earliest decades of Christianity. Ideologically, they were dualists. They believed that there were two very different aspects of the world: material and spiritual. A Christian's responsibility was to avoid the material aspects of life and focus instead on recovering the divine light inside themselves, which is obscured by all in human life that is inevitably earthy, beginning with birth from a mother's womb. The material (bad) always taints the spiritual (good), the Cathars said, so they sought to separate themselves from things of this earth. If they had taken their beliefs only that far, Peter Damian and Peter Morrone would have agreed with this kind of dualism, but the Cathars went further, adding layers onto Christian orthodoxy. In Catharist thought, the earth (and all things material) were the creation of a lesser but nonetheless divine

God, known commonly as Satan, and it was Satan's rule of earthly existence that made it necessary for Christians to remove themselves from contact with everything that was not of the pure mind and spirit.

The Cathars' dualism was metaphysical, as well. They believed that all human souls originate in heaven and fall to earth, only to be clothed, fatefully and unfortunately, in bodies. Made up of physical matter and thereby naturally corrupt, the human bodies are controlled ultimately by the evil one. Our human lives, the Cathars believed, are characterized by a struggle between God and the evil one, between the spiritual world of purity and the material world of evil and sin. Theologically, they found some justification for these beliefs in the fourth gospel, the one that says nothing of the Son of Man being born of a woman, and instead offers that "the Word became flesh and dwelt among us, full of grace and truth; we have beheld his glory" (Jn. 1:14).

Spiritually, they were like the Waldensians and others before them, advocating a mendicant life as the only true way of following Christ. The Catharist Christ was not so much a man as he was a serene and luminous piece of heaven, a triumph over evil and darkness. Since matter itself was the cause of evil, all contact with matter—anything experienced by the five senses—was an obstacle to be overcome. The Cathars denied that God was the Creator of all things, arguing that the origins of evil are separated from the origins of all that comes from God and is good. The Cathars were intellectual people, for the most part, and their ideas spread into ascetic, ethical imperatives: chastity for everyone, no marriage, no ownership of property (for nothing good could ever be owned); even suicide was sometimes seen as a logical choice.

Politically, the Cathars were a thorn in the side of the papacy, preaching that all should repent, including the holy father—and sometimes *primarily* him! They took the drive for reform further than any of the other groups had done. They generally despised the clergy, seeing them as the epitome of all of the problems in the churches. Pope Innocent III fought this conflagration of beliefs and practices with all of his ability, even declaring a formal crusade against the Cathars in southern France in 1209 (the year of Peter's birth). As a result many Cathars fled their footholds in the mountains and many made their way to similar locations in Italy and elsewhere. Peter would come into contact with many Cathars during his seven decades in the Abruzzi mountains. In the nearby town of Verona, for example, 174 of them were burned at the stake for their beliefs in 1274.[6] That was the year that Peter traveled to Lyon to attend the ecumenical council.

Evil Incarnate

All of these obsessions with salvation were fueled above all by a preoccupation with the possibility that evil might settle in one unique person—a person of evil intent, or what the First and Second Epistles of John call an "antichrist." Such a one may be among us, many thought. The Pseudepigraphal *Ascension of Isaiah,* written late in the first century or early in the second, was the first Christian text to identify a specific person as the antichrist—specifically, the emperor Nero. Saint Augustine of Hippo famously wrote in the *City of God:* "It is uncertain in what temple the antichrist will sit, whether in the ruin of the temple that was built by Solomon, or in the Church." By then, it had become common to look for the antichrist, or at least to see signs of his presence. Just as people looked fervently for an ideal leader, they also tried to sniff out those who might tear down the body of Christ.

During Peter's era religious leaders would accuse each other of being evil incarnate on a regular basis. Even royal leaders occasionally resorted to using the label as an epithet, suggesting that a rival's actions might indicate some deeper, more sinister, plan. Frederick II Hohenstaufen was often referred to as an antichrist, or as the evil one's forerunner, in papal encyclicals in the 1240s, a sign, it was said, that the end of the world was approaching. The encroaching Mongols on the eastern edge of the Western Empire, and fiery passages from the apocalyptic predictions of Joachim of Fiore (ca. 1135–1202), added logs to these blazing verbal fires.[7] Within the family of faith, the word *antichrist* was sometimes thrown about as well, as when the Prince-Archbishop of Salzburg accused Pope Gregory IX at a church council in 1241 of being the antichrist because of his claims to infallibility. Even the founder of modern empiricism, Roger Bacon, declared that the antichrist might be walking around in the world in the middle of the thirteenth century. But the most popularly believed candidate for the infamous title remained Emperor Frederick II, until he died in 1250. Then the suspicion was cast on others. And then others. "All wise men believe," Bacon ominously wrote, "that we are not far removed from the time of antichrist."[8]

Philosophers and astronomers also got in on the act, predicting when Satan would rise up and the world would enter its tumultuous period before the end, when true believers would finally be known for certain and nonbelievers cast off. Bacon looked forward to the day when Islam would finally be conquered. He didn't believe that the evil one would be outrageous or conspicuous; on the contrary, he seemed to see an antichrist who would be created in his own image. He wrote: "Antichrist will use the discoveries of science to crush and confound the power of this world."[9] Intriguingly, Bacon calculated when this period would begin by looking to astrology as interpreted by Muslim theologians. According to such principles, Bacon concluded that Islam would fall, leaving a vacuum for a uniquely evil personage in Islam's 693rd year: 1294 C.E.

So on the one hand people were searching for signs of the ultimate human incarnation of evil; and on the other, they were seeking someone who might be messiah-like and lead all things toward goodness. The reformist energy of the Humiliati, Waldensians, and Cathars was evident in nearly every town and city in Western Europe and was aimed at discovering what was pure about Christian faith, and creating leaders who could lead the Church back into the messianic era promised by Christ. These two missions were coming quickly to a head at the time when Peter was chosen pope.

One More Forerunner

Only a century earlier, the aforementioned enigmatic Joachim of Fiore had left his place in the Cistercian hierarchy to found an order of penitents in the mountains, becoming the most significant prophet of the century before Peter Morrone. By Peter's time, Joachim's teachings were known all over the Christian world.

A controversial figure, Joachim was revered by many but scorned by the serious thinkers of his day. Both Thomas Aquinas and Bonaventure were his contemporaries, and neither gave the man or his ideas the time of day. Despite his medieval prominence, he remains an outsider even today. In a sermon delivered in 2009, Pope Benedict XVI's preacher to the papal household, Father Raniero Cantalamessa, found it necessary to restate the official position of the Church that Joachim was a heretic. Dante, of course (always the contrarian), loved this man of the people and placed him in *Paradiso*.

Joachim was highly critical of his Church. He was like "an enigmatic oracle foretelling woes, especially on Rome,"[10] preaching and writing of a more democratic religious future in which ecclesiastical hierarchy would one day become unnecessary. As a monk and hermit he traveled from hill town to valley city, simultaneously sparking interest and then seeking to avoid the growing crowds of admirers and emulators who sought him out. It's probably not an accident that our hermit resembles this prophet who was known to many as the "oracle of Calabria." Peter knew Joachim's writings and studied his ideas.

A century before Peter, Joachim left his order in order to found a new, stricter, community. Later in both men's lives each desired no longer to be abbots. Charismatic and capable men were usually chosen to run things, and running a monastery involves a variety of responsibilities. Abbots were required to consider the most mundane things. Who would cook and clean? Who was in charge of milking the goats? These day-to-day details were little more than annoyances to men like Joachim and Peter, who preferred to focus on preaching, teaching, and prayer.

Joachim was also a fierce critic of one of the most popular theological ideas of his age, posited by Peter Lombard in the *Four Books of Sentences,* a book that every religious student had to study. The idea was that the Godhead, in the purest and most ideal sense, couldn't ever possibly be known in this world. God could be contemplated but never truly understood. Joachim disagreed, insisting that God wanted to be known in history, in the workings of the world in each era. He interpreted Scripture allegorically, identifying a variety of passages that speak of a new, idealized era and believed that humankind was standing on its threshold. He claimed special revelation. Joachim believed that he was the recipient of apocalyptic insight—messages from God delivered in the form of words to his mind and pen. A new day was at hand, and God had told him so.

Joachim was granted privileges by the people who were drawn to his teachings and by monks who desired his uncommon wisdom. He did a lot of teaching, employing secretaries to copy down his many theories. The resulting body of work was a philosophy that interpreted all of human history. In 1190 or 1191 he first articulated his abstruse prophecies, dividing Christian history into three distinct epochs.

The first era was characterized by the reign of God the Father, during the period of God's chosen people as told in the Hebrew Bible, when law was the rule and obedience the response. The second era was typified by the advent of God the Son—the story told in the Gospels—with grace and faith governing. But it's the third era of Joachim's apocalyptic vision that most concerns us. It was the era that preoccupied the young Peter Morrone. Peter believed that the Joachimite third era had begun in his own day. According to Joachim, it would be a time when God the Holy Spirit would reign and when fear would be replaced by brotherly love, creating the setting for the life of the world to come. The Age of Spirit was upon the thirteenth century; it was "the great Sabbath to come at the end of the world," as Joachim taught his followers.[11] Any spiritual teacher who counseled others on personal repentance, spiritual asceticism, and reform walked in this well-worn path. Any reformer might be the one to usher in this great and final era.

It was in this context that Christians dreamed of a more heavenly future when a holy father might bring peace and order to a chaotic world, in which good could overcome evil, even though good was not as easy to find. Popular in the imagination was the idea of an ideal spiritual father, a blessed pope who would bring Christ's kingdom to earth. Perhaps their century might eventually reveal "revolutionary change from corruption and ruin to spiritual revival through the revelation of a savior-ruler."[12] This idealized figure was commonly called *papa angelico,* angelic father.

So many popes in history had acted with indifference or downright hostility toward the faithful that the concept of papa angelico expressed the expectation that one man would be different. He would save the Holy Catholic Church from its obvious faults and lead the world into a more heavenly future. As Roger Bacon was known to say, the world was in such a state of disarray, with evil intentions holding sway over good, that either the antichrist would come or else one who was good and who had power—like a holy pope—would make himself known. This wasn't exactly a messianic expectation, but it *was* the promise of an ideal human ruler who would govern without self-interest. It was thought that such a figure would bring peace to the world in a way that would prepare human-kind for the Second Coming of Christ.

RIDING ON AN ASS

After the papal election of 1294, when the Church authorities came for him, Peter, by then eighty-four years old, must have thought that he would never return, that he would never again be able to live quietly on his mountain. Every pope before him had died in office. That's what popes do. They lead the world's Church. They minister. They die. It's all part of the job.

Yet Peter wasn't the only one with a sense of foreboding. Many saw a negative omen when one month and five days after the election Cardinal Latino Malabranca died. The dean of the cardinals who had nominated the new pope was taken by God before the new era could even begin.

Peter probably dreaded the journey to as far away a place as Perugia. There the cardinals expected him to come so that he could be invested as pope. But Peter's days of journeying were over. So instead Charles II told him that he should choose his own place of coronation, encouraging him of course to remain within the Kingdom of

Naples. Insiders within the papal curia were already growing suspicious. Why were the Neapolitans surrounding the
new holy father? Why did Peter seem to have no interest
in consulting with the cardinals on important matters of
transition? Signs seemed to be mounting that the Sacred
College had made a mistake.

Whatever agreement was made between Peter and
Charles II, the hermit would not be inaugurated as pope
in Rome. He was to stay in Charles's kingdom. By mid-
August, after a month of waiting, the cardinals began giving up hope that Peter would come to them in Perugia,
from where they all would have made a procession to
St. John Lateran, the cathedral church in Rome where
Saint Peter himself once celebrated Mass on the high altar.
This was the *sancta sanctorum* of Christianity, where the
most sacred objects, offerings, vessels, and sanctuary of
Christ were kept, equivalent to the "holy of holies" of the
ancient Temple in Judaism.[1] Sitting adjacent to the Basilica
of St. John Lateran on the Piazza San Giovanni is the Apostolic Palace of the Lateran, which had been the primary
residence of popes since the fourth century. Instead of
proceeding as they had expected, the cardinals began
making their way one by one to L'Aquila, a place that
some of them had never before visited.

Sitting close to the Apennine mountains, a town surrounded on all sides by peaks, L'Aquila is cool by comparison to other cities in central Italy. A reporter for the British
Catholic weekly *The Tablet* recently characterized the place
this way:

> It's a chilly place, L'Aquila, at the best of times.
> The historic city, its centre a maze of narrow

medieval streets opening on to graceful piazzas, lies
on a mountainside at an altitude of over 2,000 feet,
wedged between no less than four snow covered
peaks rising to more than 6,000 feet. Locals like to
joke that L'Aquila enjoys 11 cold months, and one
cool month, which is called summer.[2]

The city hadn't been a place of importance for very
long. In the 1240s Holy Roman Emperor Frederick II
made it Abruzzo's capital, building on what were then
much smaller villages. Wealth poured into the town and
infrastructure boomed. The prestige L'Aquila gained led
to unwanted attention, and the city would be ravaged by
competitors to the emperor's throne, only to be restored
and thoroughly protected by Charles I of Anjou, when he
ultimately brought Frederick II's reign in Italy to an end.
To many of the people in the region, a papal coronation
in their midst was a sign that the Church was finally recog-
nizing the southern peoples of Italy. They had been dominated by emperors of the north for too long, and even a
Roman pope would not have represented the savior that
this southern pope did.

Peter's coronation ceremony took place in L'Aquila
on August 29, 1294, at the Basilica of Santa Maria of
Collemaggio, the church that he'd built only a decade earlier. As was often the case when Peter seemed to be acqui-
escing to the wishes of Charles II, it is not simply the case
that he was easily convinced to be the first pope crowned
outside of Rome. The new pontiff also enjoyed the idea of
staying close to home, and he insisted on beginning his
reign as a pope of the people. Peter wanted to be crowned
at home among his spiritual brothers. Perhaps he also

wanted to emphasize that he was more than just the lord of Rome. He would lead a Church that was decentralized politically, and spiritually more universal.

As many as 200,000 people attended the celebration. Legend has it that Dante Alighieri was in the crowd. By 1294 the great Florentine poet was a close associate of Charles Martel of Anjou, the one who had walked Peter down Morrone. Hopes were high for the future of Christ's kingdom on earth now that it was in the hands of such a man as Peter.

He took the name Celestine, which means "heavenly one." In some ways Celestine's coronation ceremony looked like many others before it. Throngs of people lined the streets to watch as incense bearers, archbishops and bishops, cardinals, and abbots and monks processed. There was festive music from the region, a lushly prepared altar in the church, and a papal seat upon which Peter would sit. Symbols of imperial power were everywhere—as they had been at papal ceremonies ever since the emperor Constantine insisted that red cape, tiaras, and white horses mark such occasions, just as they did the coronations of Roman emperors. Constantine gave to Pope Sylvester I (314–35) and, by extension, each of his successors, permission to be invested in their office with full use of imperial regalia and ritual. This included processions, guards of honor, ceremonial costume, attendants from among the most noble men and the imperial militia, to the acclamation of all the citizens of the empire. With rare exception, this is what followed in papal ceremonies from the fourth century until the fourteenth.[3]

In the case of Peter, the man who followed this magnificent train was not being carried aloft like a king under a canopy; he wasn't riding on a splendid white steed. He was aloft a simple donkey whose reins were held by the king of Naples.

Saint Francis and the Spirituals

The people in the crowd that day were shocked by the symbolism of Peter's conveyance, and began to ask each other for more information about this unusual pontiff. They knew him by reputation, and some had met Peter in brief moments upon Maiella or Morrone or as he passed through their cities. Perhaps some were also his Angelerio relatives: cousins, or the children, grandchildren, and great-grandchildren of his siblings. All of those present watched Celestine's every move. To see this pope's hands and feet was to see his age and a lifetime of physical asceticism; his hands were misshapen and calloused like those of a farmer and his toes curled up like those of a dancer, from many decades of asking much of them. There was no doubt that something unusual was happening, and it wasn't lost on the crowd that an event like this had never before been held in such a humble place.

As the people watched the procession of this old monk on a donkey, some must have thought of Saint Francis of Assisi. As we glimpsed in the last chapter, people believed that "the new world of the Spirit was to be built on the final ruin of the old, and the mendicant orders were to be its prophets."[4] The most influential of these orders were the Franciscans.

As a young man, Francis heard a sermon preached on a text from Matthew's Gospel—and he took it literally. The text reads:

And preach as you go, saying, "The kingdom of heaven is at hand." Heal the sick, raise the dead, cleanse lepers, cast out demons. You received without pay, give without pay. Take no gold, nor silver, nor copper in your belts, no bag for your journey, nor two tunics, nor sandals, nor a staff [Mt. 10:7–10].

A spoiled, highborn young man, he changed his entire life upon hearing these words. He zeroed in on each of the phrases as if Jesus was speaking directly to his heart. He devoted himself to others and to a life of literal poverty. Francis's movement began with a handful of followers, mostly uneducated men, who were required to give away all of their belongings to neighbors and friends and to imitate Jesus. Francis and his brothers often showed themselves as more humble than the religious authorities around them, and their way of life was a self-conscious critique upon the social structures of Francis's day. Italy and all of Europe were transformed by his movement within a decade. By 1217 tens of thousands of men and women were counted among the Franciscans, and their numbers were large enough that they could send members to Spain, France, and the Middle East, founding provinces in each of these places.

Francis created the "friar," a man who worked outside the cloister, with the people, preached in the streets and city squares, begged for his daily bread, and lived joyfully without concern for the morrow. But within a generation the friars fell into disrepute. With wicked humor Boccaccio would summarize the perceptions of the common people of Italy in one of the stories in the *Decameron*, first published in 1353:

There was once a time when friars were saintly and worthy men, but those who claim the title and reputation of a friar today are nothing like the friars of old—except for in the clothes they wear. No, even the habits they wear are inauthentic, because those who invented them said that they should be tight, coarse, shabby, and humble, showing the disdain that a friar feels for the things of this world. But today's "friars" wear flowing gowns, smooth, pontifical habits, and they strut like peacocks in our churches and city streets showing them off.

What happened?

Within a few years of Francis's death, his followers were deeply divided between those who wanted to remain absolutely faithful to the founder's teachings about poverty—they were called the "Spirituals"—and those who viewed Francis's instructions as more temporary—they were called the "Conventuals." The latter was by far the larger of the two groups, consisting of the leaders of the order, including all but one of its ministers-general since the saint's death in 1226. Nicholas IV, the Franciscan pope whose death left the vacancy that Peter filled, was a former minister-general and a Conventual. As often happens in such cases, the two sides tended to move to the ideological extreme edges of their positions.

Francis had raised awareness of the role of money in the Church (its uses and abuses) to new heights: He taught his followers that they weren't even to handle it. Money was never to be in their pockets. They were never to accept it, store it, bank it, or use it. This was a radical step and one that he believed had been inaugurated by Jesus himself. And even before Francis's death the Franciscans were

divided between those who would follow this teaching to
the letter, and those who would interpret it metaphorically.

Francis foresaw that faithfulness to his Rule would become an issue of contention between his brethren. He
wrote: "I, Brother Francis, firmly command and decree
that no one delete or add to what has been written in this
life. The brothers may have no other Rule."[5] But the Conventuals came to believe that at least popes could add to or
alter their Rule. If a holy father couldn't do so, what did it
mean that Christ gave Saint Peter the power to loose and
to bind? But the Spirituals, who sought to retain the ideals
of Saint Francis, remained implacable. They went so far as
to say that popes who acted to change the Rule to suit the
Conventuals were acting against the Gospel of Christ and
therefore had lost their papal authority.[6]

The dominant voice of the Spirituals, Angelo Clareno (1247–1337), liked to depict Christ speaking directly
to Francis of Assisi, as if Angelo himself had been privy
to their conversations. In one vision or account, Angelo
depicts Christ appearing to Francis and speaking in the
context of Joachimite prophecy: "I have asked my father
to give me in this last hour a particular kind of people,
namely poor, humble, gentle, and mild persons. This people should be in everything like me in poverty and humility." Christ then instructs the Franciscans on how to live in
the ways of poverty—ways that the Spirituals believed they
were modeling perfectly:

> [Y]ou and all the brothers whom I will give to you,
> living like foreigners and pilgrims dead to the world
> in my likeness, ought to establish yourselves, your
> Rule and your life on the poverty and the nudity of
> my cross. . . . The places where . . . the brothers will

dwell in order to worship and praise me should be
vile, impoverished, built of sticks and mud, segre-
gated from the tumults and vanities of the world,
and free from any right of ownership.[7]

This is personal revelation for political purposes par
excellence.

Mainstream Conventual Franciscans had many reasons
to be suspicious of the Spirituals. Spirituals were accused
by Conventuals of being dissenters and defectors who were
tearing apart a beautiful movement because they believed
they knew best the intentions of their famous founder.
The dispute about poverty was not simply theological. It
often resulted in ugly and violent episodes. There were
cases when Conventuals tortured their brother Franciscans in order to force recantations, and such events were
witnessed throughout Italy during Peter's time. News of
these struggles and atrocities traveled rapidly in religious
circles—even up into the mountains where hermits lived.
It is even likely that Spirituals spent time hiding out in the
caves of Peter and his brethren.

As Peter rode to the Basilica of Santa Maria of Collemaggio on August 29, 1294, for his coronation, he carried
himself with great humility, insisting on being treated no
better than his Lord, who had ridden into Jerusalem on
an ass. But was that all it was? Was this also an example of
his power?

To the medieval imagination, a man with a reputation
for sanctity communicated a superior, lasting, eternal en-
dowment that could not be matched by the most stately
regal authority. Peter's early decision to make his identity

known in this way—as more of a holy man than a pope—
may actually be an example of a pope who carefully crafted
his image.

Pope Celestine would not be like the men who had
come before him. The cardinals, curia, and ecclesiastics in
Italy, as well as the princes and kings at home and abroad,
watched carefully for the direction of this new papacy.

The contrast between the life this man had led and the
office he now held was unmistakable. The people lining
the streets of L'Aquila were witnessing a man already showing signs of "going his own way."

More Symbols

We don't know what Peter was thinking on that day. He left
no diary behind. Perhaps he also thought of the fourth-
century Saint Martin of Tours. When the bishop of Poitiers
wanted to ordain Martin he insisted that it be to the lowest
possible rank. He thus became an exorcist. Martin began
to live like a hermit, and people would come from long
distances to seek his counsel. Eventually a community grew
up around him, much to Martin's disappointment. Then
when the bishop of Tours died, the diminutive Martin was
pressed to accept the job of bishop. He agreed, but only if
he could sit on a wooden stool in the cathedral and not in
the bishop's ornate chair. Throughout his time as bishop,
Martin refused to ride a horse or be driven in a chariot. He
also rode a donkey.

In contrast, older Catholics today might remember the
last great papal ceremony, that of John XXIII in 1958 in
St. Peter's Square. It lasted the traditional five hours and

was full of the pageantry that used to be common for the holy fathers. John XXIII was crowned with tiaras made specifically for the occasion, encrusted with jewels, and paraded like a king through Rome. Such celebrations were abolished by the Second Vatican Council. Most recently, Pope Benedict XVI did not include an actual coronation in his installation ceremony.

In the basilica, a pallium was placed upon Celestine's shoulders. A pallium is a narrow strip of white lamb's wool with black crosses woven into a design that was intended to be worn solely by popes. (The 1431 Council of Basel would condemn the practice of popes' granting their palliums to their cronies.) Only three cardinals were in attendance at Celestine's investiture, because only three had arrived by the time the ceremony began since Charles II insisted that the installation move forward. As one historian has written, it all appeared as if Charles "t[ook] the simple old man into honorable custody."[8] Speculation swirled that Charles wanted the ceremony wrapped up before the cardinals could gather again and try to change their minds. Charles II's haste was later remedied; as a compromise the whole ceremony was repeated for the sake of the rest of the Sacred College several days later. Celestine V's is the only instance in history of a double papal coronation.

In addition to the pallium, every pope was invested with other symbols of his power as both supreme religious leader and head of state, including the sacred mantle or coat (scarlet, to match the ancient color of the imperial monarch's garment), a tiara upon his head, the Fisherman's gold ring on his finger connecting him to the lineage of Saint Peter, the triple cross, and the crossed keys—to heaven.

Consider the tiara, encrusted with jewels. This piece

of liturgical gear was designed to set the pope apart from every other bishop and leader of the Church, marking him as the supreme monarch on earth. The placing of the crown on the pope's head was accompanied by the following symbolic words: "Receive the tiara and know that thou art Father of princes and kings, Ruler of the world, Vicar of our Savior Jesus Christ." It wasn't long before ruling sultans of the Ottoman Empire were having their own three-tiered, and then four-tiered, tiaras made for their own coronations. Celestine V's tiara didn't match well the ass he rode in on, but it was at least less ostentatious than the "double crown" of his successor, Boniface VIII, and the "triple crown" that would sit on Clement V's head in 1305. In recent memory, Pope John Paul II also refused to wear the tiara, reflecting in his inauguration homily: "This is not the time to return to a ceremony and an object considered, wrongly, to be a symbol of the temporal power of the Popes. Our time calls us, urges us, obliges us to gaze on the Lord and immerse ourselves in humble and devout meditation on the mystery of the supreme power of Christ himself."

After the crown was placed on Peter's head, the cardinals and princes would have knelt and kissed his sandaled feet.

Consider, too, the crossed keys that are featured so prominently in papal regalia and insignia. One is made of gold, and the other of silver; they are always pictured bound together by a red cord. The crossed keys symbolize the power to open the gates of heaven, as is shown in two verses from the Bible, the first from a prophecy of the Messiah, and the second from the words of Jesus to his disciples:

And I will place on his shoulder the key of the
house of David; he shall open, and none shall shut;
he shall shut, and none shall open. (Is. 22:22)

I will give you the keys of the kingdom of heaven,
and whatever you bind on earth shall be bound in
heaven, and whatever you loose on earth shall be
loosed in heaven. (Mt. 16:19)

We don't know how Celestine felt about these symbols,
only that he endured them. They would have been largely
unfamiliar to him, as he'd never been a member of the
curia or even a bishop or cardinal.

Chief among all papal symbols of authority is the Chair
of St. Peter. Since the late Renaissance, the apostle's famous
chair has been enclosed in a tall gilt bronze casing created
by the Renaissance sculptor Gian Lorenzo Bernini, and it
stands in the middle of St. Peter's Basilica. It is one of the
most popular tourist attractions, visited by thousands of
visitors each day. Before Bernini designed the casing, the
chair was more than a symbol; it was an actual relic. At the
time of Celestine V's coronation, many believed the Chair
of St. Peter was the very chair sat upon by the saint himself
in the first century. (We now know that the chair within
the enormous and ornate Bernini structure was a gift of
Charles the Bald to Pope John VIII in 875 c.e.)

The Bernini chair sits within an apse that has these
verses inscribed in gold lettering, in Latin:

And I tell you, you are Peter, and on this Rock, I
will build my Church, and the gates of Hades shall
not prevail against it. I will give you the keys of the

kingdom of heaven, and whatever you bind on earth
shall be bound in heaven, and whatever you loose
on earth shall be loosed in heaven. (Mt. 16:18–19)

This is a chair upon which Celestine V never sat. This pope
would never make it to Rome.

13

THE COLORFUL KINGS OF NAPLES
AND SICILY

Spiritual movements were not all that was convulsing Western Europe at the time of Peter's coronation. The lives of two kings of Sicily, a father and a son, neither of them Italian, were entangled with Peter Morrone before and after his election as holy father.

In 1294 the struggles of popes to assert both spiritual and temporal power over other rulers were intensely felt. A pope was also a king; his sacred calling was to hold *regnum* (royal) as well as *sacerdotium* (priestly) power. Yet the divine right of kings was a more ancient idea than the divine right of popes. Kings have been ordained for as long as clergy have been, and long before Christ ever walked the earth. The king of France, for instance, argued that his predecessors had been recognized as "protectors" of Christendom before there had ever been popes. Similarly, King Edward I of England, who ruled simultaneously with Celestine V, argued that England and Scotland were founded by Brutus of Troy (a legendary figure) more than a millennium before Christ. The ancient psalmist sings of a God "who is to be feared, who cuts off the spirit of princes, who is awesome to the kings of the earth"—but it is God who does these things, not man (Ps. 76:11–12). As pope, Peter would have no choice but to work closely with kings both good and bad.

The struggle between kings and religious leaders is as old as the stories of the prophet Samuel arguing with Saul, the first king of Israel, 3,000 years ago as told in the Hebrew Bible. The prophet was the one to anoint the king, signaling that the king's leadership was according to the desire of God. But soon after Saul came to power the regal and the priestly clashed. God refused to answer the inquiries of Saul in 1 Samuel 28 and then responded immediately and even audibly to the next-appointed ruler, David (in 1 Samuel 30:8 and elsewhere). And the prophet knew what would happen all along.

Kings had a sacred duty to provide order and security so that their people could pursue lives without undue fear or want. In their work, the royal and religious were also commingled. The first Roman emperors—Julius Caesar and Augustus (100 B.C.E.–14 C.E.)—were widely deified by their people, sometimes even before they were dead; they were regarded as *divus* (deified ones), gods who had started out as men. By the Middle Ages, worship of a *divus* sovereign was less common, but many an ancient and medieval king was believed to carry powers of healing through his touch or by a glance—like a pope, like a saint. It was believed that there was a divine authority for kings that, many believed, came from God alone. There could be no legitimate earthly challengers to such a sovereign's rule—even popes.

When the emperor Constantine declared Christianity the religion of state in 313 C.E., he didn't need a pope to crown him. In those days, the role of the emperor was far stronger than the papacy. Once the empire began to disintegrate in confusion in the early fifth century, the papacy took on a greater and greater role in world affairs. Historian Eamon Duffy explains it this way: "As the Roman Empire collapsed, and the barbarian nations arose to fill the vacuum, the popes, in default of any other agency, set themselves to shape the destiny of the West, acting as midwives to the emergence of Europe, creating emperors, deposing monarchs for rebellion against the Church."[1] The first prominent pope to create an emperor would be Leo III. He crowned the German-born Charlemagne the first Holy Roman Emperor on December 25, 800. From Charlemagne on, the model of Samuel's relationship to Saul and David became the papal model and ideal for authority. It was a tradition that the Holy See attempted to continue. All leadership—secular and religious—would flow from Christ's vicar.

But every pope was different, and Celestine V showed less appetite for ruling than had his predecessors. Meanwhile, Charles II was keen for power. So as Peter was overwhelmed by the decision of the cardinals, trying to understand what his new role would be, Charles was behind the scenes maneuvering.

Charles I and the Italian Peninsula

Charles II was the child of Charles I of Anjou, who was in turn the son of King Louis VIII of France, member of the House of Capet, hereditary rulers of France since 987 C.E. Born in 1226, Charles I had several older brothers and thus stood to inherit nothing from his illustrious father. His eldest brother, also named Louis, was twelve years his senior and became King Louis IX when their father died within a year of Charles's birth. Louis would become the first and only French king to be canonized by the Catholic Church. The piety of Saint Louis IX was legendary; many of his subjects believed him to be a reincarnation of Jesus Christ. Louis washed the feet of the poor, fed the hungry at his royal table, acquired a highly prized relic—the crown of thorns that supposedly adorned the head of Christ—and placed it in the glorious Sainte-Chapelle in Paris. He died in 1270 while lying on a bed of ashes in order to demonstrate the frailty of man. It would be difficult to follow such a brother.

Charles I wasn't so pious. And he wasn't as lucky. In those days, the practice of apanage meant that vast swathes of territory were granted to younger male children so that they would have something to rule and rely upon in lieu of an inheritance, since everything was entailed to the eldest son. Charles didn't receive his apanage, nor was his brother Philippe's transferred to Charles after Philippe died at the age of ten. It seems that Charles was the least favored of all of his siblings. But by 1247 he was made Count of Anjou by his saintly brother, King Louis, and with determination he eventually became both the model crusader and the perfect knight, according to contemporary accounts.[2] He was anxious to prove himself.

Frederick Rolfe once called the Italy of the late Middle Ages "not a nation, but a geographical expression." Its land ranged from the Alps to the tip of the peninsula, "the boot," that nearly touches Africa, and also included the two largest islands in the Mediterranean Sea. There was a multitude of competing powers battling for control of these lands, from smallish bands of mercenaries to large kingdoms led by lords and princes. For more than seven hundred years, beginning in about 1130, all of southern Italy passed from ruler to ruler under the governance of a king in an area that was then called the Kingdom of Sicily, the Kingdom of Naples, and sometimes the Kingdom of Sicily and Naples. Spanish, Norman, German, and French royals ruled. Princes and kings from the north and west had been visiting, conquering, and occupying the lands of the Italian peninsula since at least the tenth century.

Meanwhile, successive popes had been anxious to free southern Italy from the clutches of the Germanic peoples who had increasingly come to control everything south of Rome. By 1260 Pope Urban IV had offered the territory of Sicily to nearly every prince or would-be king who promised to expel the Hohenstaufen emperors from the peninsula. As one historian has explained, "The popes were generally in alliance with the kings of France, on the basis of mutual hostility to the emperor in Germany and northern Italy, though that did not always prevent conflict between them."[3]

Finally, in 1266, with the help of Urban IV's successor, Pope Clement IV, Charles I took control of the Italian peninsula and the last of the Hohenstaufens—Manfred, son of Frederick II—was ousted. Both pope and king spoke of their victory over the Germans as a true liberation of the Italian people. Charles would also go on to conquer land along the Adriatic seaboard, and in 1272 he named himself king of Albania, as well.

Once he began to rule these lands, Charles I visited and sometimes contributed to the monastic orders and abbeys throughout Molise and the Abruzzi. Sometime in the 1270s both father and son probably first met Peter Morrone. In

1277, for example, Charles I sponsored a French Cistercian monastery near Mount Morrone, on lands owned by Charles not far from Peter's mountain retreat; he named it Santa Maria della Vittoria (Blessed Virgin Mary of the Victory). The harvests of the surrounding fields would go to support the monks' needs. In turn, the French monks would pray for Charles's soul and the souls of all who had died in the holy cause of his victories. The new ruler's ambitions seemed to know few bounds. Charles even had designs on Constantinople and took part in Crusades with that object in mind, but never with any success.

Enter the Son, Charles II

A few years later, the Kingdom of Sicily—which extended from the southern suburbs of Rome to the bottom of Italy, including the island—became embroiled in a war known as the Sicilian Vespers. The conflict began the day after Easter, March 30, 1282. The Sicilian people rebelled against the rule of that same king, Charles I, who had liberated them from the Germans. Unlike the Hohenstaufens, Charles I ruled with the support of the papacy, but just like the Germans he employed soldiers and mercenaries who often pillaged and stole, even raped and tortured, in order to bring the people into submission. And he taxed the people just as the Hohenstaufens had done: excessively. Things were no better for the average Sicilian under Charles's rule than they had been under the Germans'.

It began at vespers (evening prayer) on Easter Monday at the Church of the Holy Spirit in Palermo. A scuffle broke out between a French officer and an Italian woman who was ignoring his advances, and soon Sicilian men began to cry out, "Death to the French!" A riot ensued. As historian Steven Runciman has described the scene,

> At once the streets were filled with angry armed men. . . . . Every Frenchman they met was struck down. They poured into the inns frequented by the French and the houses where they dwelt, sparing neither man, woman nor child. Sicilian girls who had married Frenchmen perished with their husbands. The rioters broke into the Dominican and Franciscan convents; and all the foreign friars were dragged out and told to pronounce the word *ciciri*, whose sound the French tongue could never accurately reproduce. Anyone who failed the test was slain.

What began as a localized insurrection at sunset blossomed into an all-out rebellion on the island, and at least 2,000 Frenchmen in Sicily died within the first twenty-four hours.[4]

Within days rebels were either inspired or recruited throughout the island and any signs of empire were attacked. Some of the rebels set fire to Charles's fleet sitting in the harbor. The Sicilians sent emissaries to the pope asking that they answer only to him, and not to another king.

This was a time for Charles II to try to be like his father. Born in 1254, Charles "was a strange contrast to his father: a frail man, slightly lame, no warrior," not a fighter or particularly good military strategist.[5] The most decisive battle of the Sicilian conflict would take place on the high seas where, at the age of thirty, Charles II led a naval party that his father intended to protect the city of Naples—

their center of power in the kingdom—from the rebels and their allies. In what is known as the battle of the Gulf of Naples, the younger Charles was tricked into easy defeat by a more experienced adversary, Roger of Lauria, who commanded a fleet of Aragonese-Sicilian ships. A tall, fearsome man, Lauria had an unparalleled influence over his men. From oarsmen to archers, he trained his men to be swift and strong, relying less on armor and more on cunning and ability. Charles II's orders were to stay in port and wait for help to arrive. Instead, he led the Neopolitan ships out in pursuit of the Sicilian ships—which is what Lauria and his men were hoping he would do. The impetuous and inexperienced Charles chased Lauria southward. Lauria pretended to retreat, only to turn and face Charles's forces upon reaching Castlelammare, where a dozen other Sicilian vessels lay in wait. It was a trap. Before the father could arrive to help from Genoa, Charles II was captured.

Failure at battle was interpreted as failure before God and the divine will. Charles II didn't possess the Spirit as his father more clearly did. Nor did he have his father's fortitude or muscle. Charles I died in 1285 "knowing that all of his careful plans and machinations were unraveling," while young Charles was still a prisoner of war.[6] Four years went by before Charles II was released, and then only by the mediation of King Edward I of England, an old friend of Charles I's from the Crusades. Charles II had lost the island of Sicily (specified in the treaty as all land "beyond the lighthouse") and retained the mainland areas, including Naples.[7]

But despite being weak in the ways that his father had been strong, Charles II more than made up for his lack of military acumen with an ability to politick. He had a way with men in power. Despite his physical ailments, he was agile of mind, patient, and skilled in the tactics of conversation and negotiation. He grew to understand the intellectual strengths and weaknesses of others. Upon being released by Peter III of Aragon, Charles II traveled to Rieti, where he met with Pope Nicholas IV. There he entered into a negotiation with Nicholas whereby Charles would be declared king of Sicily—taking back the full territory in name if not in reality. In 1289 he also convinced the pope to excommunicate the Aragonese leader whom Charles then "deposed." (That Aragonese king, Alfonso III, would later pay tribute of his own to the Holy See and be welcomed back into the fold.)

Five years went by and in 1294 we see Charles II negotiating with Peter Morrone in Sulmona, discussing with the new pope matters that were usually outside a king's purview.

Every man in history has a variety of motivations that lie hidden from easy view. Charles II was political and selfish, but he also seems to have been religiously motivated in deeper ways than his father ever was. As often happens from one generation to the next, the son does not imitate the strengths of the father but develops his own. For example, "A review of the Angevin Registers reveals numerous episodes in which Charles I was attempting to eradicate the radical Franciscans from the kingdom," yet in the next generation we know that Charles II appointed Franciscan Spirituals to tutor his three sons.[8] The eldest of his sons was the aforementioned Charles Martel, who walked Peter down the mountain. Charles Martel may have possessed even more sincere interest than his father in Peter's work. But he had little time to demonstrate it. He died tragically in Naples in 1295.

Charles's second eldest, Louis, then renounced his

right to succeed his father as king of Naples, choosing instead to become a Franciscan friar. And finally, Robert of Anjou, the third son of Charles II, became king, reigning long (1309–43) and championing the cause of the Franciscan Spirituals during his rule. All three of these sons may have been motivated toward sanctity by the example of Peter Morrone.[9]

Yet despite whatever redemption future generations can provide for their fathers and grandfathers, Dante still places both Charles I and Charles II halfway between *Paradiso* and *Inferno* in his *Divine Comedy*.[10] Eternal uncertainty is their sentence for the havoc they stirred up in thirteenth-century religion and politics. The poet even names the seventh canto of his *Purgatorio* "The Valley of the Negligent Rulers" for the negative effect that such rulers had on the Church.

FIFTEEN DISASTROUS WEEKS

One of the common explanations for why the cardinals chose Peter is that by electing an elderly and inexperienced man they thought they'd be able to rule him. They picked someone who they assumed wouldn't be much trouble for them or their allies. If that's the case, they misjudged, not because Celestine V turned out to be a strong leader, but because he was so weak that others got hold of him before the curia ever had a chance. Peter ruled for fifteen disastrous weeks from August 29 to December 13, 1294. Not a day went by when he wasn't unduly influenced—often without his knowledge—by the Neapolitan monarchs who convinced him to live among them.

In the twelve centuries since the apostle Peter became the first pope, no other pontiff had ever intended to rule the Church completely apart from the resources at his disposal in Rome. Celestine V's papacy was troubled from the start because all his early counselors were the friends of the king of Naples and his son, and Celestine ruled in cities far removed from the Eternal City, both religiously and geographically. This was his first mistake.

Avoiding Rome was not in itself unusual. In fact, bishops often felt unsafe in its unfriendly environs. Rome was an epicenter of both the Church and a republic that disliked its own bishops. Those same powerful, fighting families that controlled the issues of State and Church agreed on at least one point: they would combine forces against any bishop who might decide that some of their power belonged to him and his office. The ruling families had a variety of motivations: "The Roman citizens showed great enthusiasm for keeping in the city the papal curia and the wealth it brought with it, but they showed equal enthusiasm for expelling popes for the sake of an independent Roman republic and senate."[1]

Nevertheless, many monks and clerics of the Holy City understood the need to have the holy father nearby. St. Peter's Basilica was built upon the very site where Saint Peter was slain in about 67 C.E. There is power in the mortal remains of Saint Peter, and the Church is built upon the blood of its martyrs. Those were the spiritual arguments. Theologically and historically, the leaders of the Church believed that the *ecclesia universalis* was not only Catholic, but Roman. God had intended that his Church be guided in its Roman framework through the protection, infrastructure, and milieu of the empire. "Unlike other states, where developments took place by God's permission," writes a modern-day essayist, "the Roman Empire grew by God's direct operation."[2] Administratively, it had become clear throughout the century before Celestine V that when popes spent summers and other extended periods of time away from the Holy See, serious problems arose. One anonymous priest lamented in the decades leading up to

1294: "Let the Roman bishops learn to love the Roman City and stay in it, because popes living outside Rome seem to have the name of their dignity half complete. . . . [A]s a woman without a husband, so does the City of Rome without a pope seem to be!"[3]

These problems were arising in the late thirteenth century, when the geography of the Papal States was in flux, and the extent of the territory that a pope was ruling was not clearly defined. It would be more than seven hundred years before Vatican City would become a sovereign city-state and the bishop of Rome would be recognized by the nations of the world as a head of state. In the thirteenth century the bishop of Rome was vying for his authority against the noble families, emperors, and kings, and even sometimes the cardinals themselves. All of the bishop of Rome's territories were hotly contested and constantly changing. It wasn't until the 1929 Lateran Treaty—between the kingdom of Italy and the Holy See— that today's Vatican State was created geographically and politically, making it wholly independent of the nation of Italy that surrounds it.[4]

Perhaps these are some clues as to why Celestine stayed away from Rome, in addition to the influence that Charles II immediately had upon him. But this also means that his first and greatest mistake of judgment may have also been one of Celestine's virtues. Perhaps, the new pope thought, he could be a better papa angelico by steering clear of the privileges and trappings of Rome. In the thirteenth century, the papal office, unlike today, held not only spiritual power but also potentially earthly power. Celestine V's decision to stay out of Rome may have been a way of rejecting what the Church had become—a kingdom on earth.

As a result of this first decision, it is no surprise that many of the other early decisions Celestine V made were at the direction of his landlord, overseer, and primary confidant: Charles II. Charles was a master at telling the spiritual father what he wanted to hear. From the outset, Peter was concerned about a number of things, including the state of his brothers and the churches and oratories that he had built throughout the years. Charles tried to assuage Peter's fears by making promises. In one instance, Peter asked Charles to promise that the cardinals in the Sacred College would be safe to travel within the territory of Charles's kingdom. There had been some question on that matter during the papal election. Some of the cardinals had worried that if they entered the territory of Naples and Sicily they might not be free to leave. Charles made this vow to the pope, only to be released from it later on.

His Second Mistake

Even before his coronation the new pope was blundering. His second mistake could not be blamed on anyone other than himself. To every person who attended his coronation and went to confession Celestine V decided to offer the same heavenly reward that had previously been offered by a pope only to the holy crusaders—a plenary indulgence.

This was a very serious matter. Certain conditions were expected to be met in order to gain a plenary indulgence. The person had to be genuinely contrite of heart and holy of purpose. The first plenary indulgence had been the unprecedented offering of Pope Urban II in 1095 to every man (and usually, his entire family) who took up arms for Christendom in the First Crusade. Even though many of these commitments were made in the fervor of the moment, with men yelling out verbal commitments to the pope's emissaries as they preached in the open air, the men followed up their promises by cutting emblems of crosses out of any available white fabric and sewing them onto their clothing. Before embarking they made arrangements in the event of their death. At some point a man surely realized that he was undertaking solemn vows and serious commitments. The First Lateran Council in 1123 devoted one of its canons (number 11) to handling those converts to the holy cause who had taken up visible "crosses" without following through on the actual commitments involved: they were to be excommunicated. In contrast, Celestine V seemed to offer a pardon for sins to any bloke who undertook to walk to his one-day celebration.

The new pope seemed to believe that he should do whatever he could for his own people. The Church coffers would fill on that special day, and who would benefit more than his brethren, their churches, their families, as well as Charles II, the landlord of the kingdom? Particularly in an age when sin and eternal punishment for sin were grave matters, the new pope's offering of a plenary indulgence could be seen as making redemption and salvation into something seemingly frivolous. But any who may have questioned the move were hesitant to say anything because it was so early in Celestine's papacy.

Celestine then extended the same privilege to all who might come to the basilica at L'Aquila, in perpetuity, on the anniversary of his coronation. His bull *Inter Sanctorum Solemnia* states that he had "opened the treasury of mercy confided to him by Christ and bestowed it upon those who were truly confessed and penitent."[5]

Throughout the century, Peter had witnessed various local parishes and bishops providing indulgences for visiting their shrines and relics, and he knew that the justification for many of these favors seemed spurious. Most famous of all, especially to one who knew the Franciscans as closely as Peter did, was the case of the Portiuncula, Saint Francis's little chapel to the Virgin Mary in the valley below Assisi. During the decades that Peter spent in the mountains, there were Franciscans who claimed that in 1216 Pope Honorius III had granted a plenary indulgence to all who visited Portiuncula. They claimed that Francis himself knew of this grace and perhaps even asked for it. The debate surrounding the claim was hot in Peter's day and has been debunked since. (No document exists to prove that such an indulgence was valid—except for one written a century later by Bishop Teobald of Assisi.)[6] But could it be that Peter looked on what he believed to be valid in Assisi and wanted his own church in L'Aquila granted the same stature and prestige? His offering of a plenary indulgence lasted for only a brief while. Less than a year later the first papal bulls of his successor would undo Peter's offer, and most of the other indulgences, appointments, and promises he had made, saying that they lacked the gravity and justice expected of the head of Christ's church.

There is no question that Charles II had undue influence over this pope. Papal historian Eamon Duffy calls Celestine "the naïve stooge of the Angevin King of Naples"[7]—and indeed he was. Gifts, appointments, and indulgences were distributed indiscriminately. And Charles arranged to have the Sicilian question quickly resolved to his satisfaction, with the pope offering unflinching backing of Charles's right to rule the territory he had lost in battle. The efforts of Charles to influence Celestine became so conspicuous that some of the most powerful cardinals of the Sacred College began washing their hands of the whole affair. They began to regret what they had done on that day only a few weeks before, uttering comments that were almost treasonous. "Go with your saint, for I will not come with you, nor let the Spirit deceive me further about him," Cardinal Gaetani was heard to mutter one day as Charles II went by.[8] Meanwhile, others began to take advantage. Cardinal Hugo Aycelin, for example, was at that time the only French member of the College. He was a Dominican biblical scholar of the first order and an ally of Charles II. It would soon become clear how much his influence would grow.

As Celestine and Charles begin their journey from L'Aquila to Naples, we see them making decisions in various cities along the way throughout the month of September 1294. After a brief stay in familiar Sulmona, they arrived in Cassino, and Celestine appointed an abbot for the historic monastery founded there by Saint Benedict in 529, perhaps without even visiting Monte Cassino itself, which lies only a mile to the east. The new abbot for the historic monastery was a Hermit of St. Damian who was unknown to the monks of Monte Cassino, and soon after the change in leadership was announced many of the senior monks left in protest.

In Teano, Celestine made a man of questionable character a cardinal—without consulting anyone but those who were present that night at dinner. He created a total of twelve new cardinals on September 18, doubling the size of the Sacred College in a single day. Numbers were rarely accidental in the late Middle Ages, and it seems that Celestine believed that he was adding twelve of his own "apostles." Two of the twelve were friends and spiritual brothers of Celestine's from the mountains. Six of them were French, including two monks, the archbishop of Bourges, one of Charles II's relatives, and the chancellor of the University of Paris. Together with Charles, it was Cardinal Aycelin who made sure that the pope appointed such a number of Frenchmen. The original group of cardinals who had elected Peter was certainly not pleased, for by the time these appointments were over it was clear that Aycelin would preside over the next papal election.

To Castle Nuovo

By October 6, Celestine and Charles were on the road to Naples, their final destination. Naples was as ancient a city as Rome, and with nearly as rich a history in Christendom. Both Saint Peter and Saint Paul probably preached there, and there were catacombs where early Christians had buried their dead, just as in Rome. But Rome was the place of Nero's most infamous persecutions of Christians in 64–66 C.E. It was in Rome that Peter and Paul breathed their last, and upon their bones the Eternal City had risen amid the ruins of Isis and other ancient goddesses and gods.

Following a brief stay in Capua, the pope and his entourage finally arrived at Charles's castle on November 5. What had only been whispered as a possibility over the previous six weeks—for a holy father lives and works as Christ's representative, and doesn't answer to anyone else on earth—became a reality: Celestine took up residence at Castle Nuovo on the Bay of Naples. The great castle had been completed just twelve years earlier by Charles's father and had sat mostly unused until Charles arrived there with the pope.[9] In the weeks leading up to their arrival, Charles had sent orders home with instructions for the streets to be paved and a papal residence built.[10]

The scandal was not the fact that the pope would reside away from Rome, for many thirteenth-century popes had recently broken that ground. Gregory IX (1227–41) spent a full eight years away from Rome during his pontificate. Gregory X (1271–76) spent extended periods of time in Provence. Three consecutive holy fathers: John XXI (1276–77), Nicholas III (1277–80), and Martin IV (1281–85) spent months and years ruling from Viterbo. And Celestine V's predecessor, Nicholas IV, spent the majority of his four years as pope away from Rome in beautiful Rieti and Orvieto.[11] The controversy this time was that Christ's vicar was taking up lodgings in the home of a king.

Clearly to all, the princes ruled him. As Hamlet says to Ophelia regarding her father, Polonius: "Let the doors be shut upon him, that he may play the fool no where but in 's own house."[12]

Today Castle Nuovo feels almost deserted by the Italian government, the triumphal arch (a later architectural addition) marred by surrounding graffiti, with little of the care that usually goes into great national landmarks. But in November of 1294 the area surrounding it bustled with vendors hawking wares and ongoing construction works. All of this activity yielded conflicting aromas. There were the smells of fruit and flowers, fresh morning bread, but also barrels of fish and makeshift pens of live pigs, containers of rotting food and household garbage. Celestine lived closer to these things than he ever would have had he sat at the Lateran Palace or St. Peter's, in Rome.

The man who had long been Charles II's own chief chancellor, Bartolomeo of Capua, was appointed to control the pontifical chancery.[13] From these ecclesiastical courts, run by the hundreds of men known as the papal curia, sprang the legal profession as we know it today; it was already fully formed in medieval Italy by about 1250, the generation before Celestine V's papacy. One of the first professions to fully emerge in Western society, "[t]hey regarded themselves and their colleagues with pride (frequently mixed with self-righteousness) as an intellectual elite who deserved to enjoy power, wealth, and other privileges because what they did was difficult, demanding, and vital to the well-being of society. Advocates and doctors of law, they insisted, were every bit as essential to a community as the soldiers who protected it from its enemies."[14] Some of the papal curia came to Naples to join their leader, but the Neapolitan officers of Charles's court took up many of these ecclesiastical functions in order to see to their own interests. Celestine V was no match for them. The once formidable hermit of Maiella and Morrone had become a man strangely beholden.

The pope was in his castle with the curia upon his doorstep, dependent upon the king's good graces. Charles II's control over Celestine V had become so complete that many in the Church hierarchy and beyond began to fear that the next papal election might be controlled by the king himself. In fact, Charles was arranging for such an eventuality, encouraging Celestine to formally reinstitute Pope Gregory X's principles for conclave in *Ubi majus periculum,* the constitution approved in Lyon in 1274 decreeing that all cardinals involved in papal elections should gather within ten days in the palace where the previous pope has died. And, in this instance, the local ruler of that place—now Charles II of Naples—would act as governor and protector for all of the proceedings.

Like a Turtle in His Shell

Charles II had prepared for Celestine V a beautiful apartment that was fitting for a pope and closely reminiscent of what the new leader could have had at St. Peter's Basilica. But Celestine's stay in Charles's splendor would be brief. He was uncomfortable, to say the least.

What happened next is reminiscent of the legends of Francis of Assisi being invited to dinner at a bishop's or governor's house. A man of importance and influence, Francis was often receiving such invitations. But when faced with a sumptuous feast—which is of course what would be prepared in such circumstances—Francis would quietly leave the table and go outside to the road to beg for some bread, or some other such thing, as a way of making his point about poverty regardless of the occasion.

By the time Advent was in full swing, eleven weeks had gone by since Celestine's coronation, and he decided that he couldn't stay in his rooms any longer. He considered moving elsewhere, but instead he had a small wooden hut built within the estate. He modeled it after his cell in the Abruzzi, which probably means that some of his own monks took the primary responsibility for the work of constructing it and arranging its contents. Within a month, Celestine had relocated to what was essentially the castle basement.

There he spent his last few weeks as a pope attempting to live apart, like a turtle in his shell. Or as James Stefaneschi put it in his biographical poem, "like the pheasant that thinks itself invisible and safe when it hides its head."[15]

By twenty-first-century standards, if a few weeks went by without the pope being seen in public or mentioned in the media one might assume there were serious problems. Even fifty years ago, with television in its infancy, when more than three weeks went by without glimpses of Pope John XXIII, there was rampant speculation that he was dying. And, in fact, he was.[16] Seven hundred years ago, in 1294, the scrutiny was still intense, and no one on the outside caught sight of Celestine V for weeks.

AWKWARDNESS IN ROBES

Peter had gone down Mount Morrone like a polar bear crossing land, but he would soon come out of Naples like one helplessly floating around on a piece of ice. The confidence of the letter he had composed to Malabranca only a couple of months earlier had slowly evaporated as he entered the last four of his fifteen weeks on Saint Peter's throne.

In his *Dialogues,* Pope Gregory the Great once reflected:

> My unhappy soul languish[es] under a burden of distractions. I recall those earlier days in the monastery where I could rise above the vanities of life. But now all the beauty of that spiritual repose is gone, and the contact with worldly men and their affairs, which is a necessary part of my duties as bishop [of Rome], has left my soul defiled.[1]

These are shocking words from one of the greatest popes in history. Had Celestine V been so eloquent he might have said something similar.

Medieval popes were often coronated to the chanting of Psalm 113:7–8 in a formal part of the service of consecration that was called "sitting in the seat of dung"—only a metaphorical suggestion:

> *He raiseth up the poor out of the dust,*
> *and lifteth the needy out of the dunghill;*
> *That he may set him with princes,*
> *even with the princes of his people.*

The ideal was that a pope would be a man raised from dust to the loftiest position of authority in Christ's church, and henceforth he must remember from whence he had come. How appropriate this was, but how rare.

Celestine V attempted to establish himself between the imperial power that came with his office and the spiritual ideals of the hermitage. The experiment would soon fail. The most powerful pope of the century before Celestine, Innocent III, "threw handfuls of coins to the assembled crowd" as he was led to his coronation at the Basilica of St. John Lateran, "as a symbol of the fact that the wealth controlled by the papacy was to be used for the service of others."[2] It is possible that Celestine felt overwhelmed from the start and knew that he wasn't strong enough to do what would be required of him. Or maybe he was just suspicious.

The consummate outsider, Celestine had reasons to be wary of the people with whom he would be associating and working alongside. From the start it was his express desire to lead an *ecclesia spiritualis* (spiritual church) rather than an *ecclesia carnalis* (material church). The competition between the two filled him with great anxiety. Not a day went by when he wasn't attempting to navigate the tension of how he might live his convictions faithfully and yet still lead—and this conflict became particularly acute in his final month—from mid-November to mid-December 1294.

Unlike most of the popes that came before and after him, instead of taking earthly action Celestine V did what a good monk would have done: he prayed. Perhaps he could do nothing else. But the contrast between him and the curia, ecclesiastics, and princes was striking.

In these times, bishops and archbishops sometimes served as warriors in addition to being statesmen and religious leaders. Medieval chronicles are full of descriptions of warrior priests—men who not only held religious office, but as rulers in the Holy Roman Empire led armies into battle. Such men were heroes of the Church.[3] In stark contrast, Pope Celestine must have believed that he was the subject of those apocalyptic expectations of the people; he must have believed that he was in fact that messiah-like figure, because he was so different from what the people expected in a religious leader. The question is: how quickly did he realize that his simple intentions and holiness would do more harm than good? Surely he knew by the time he had taken up residence in the castle basement.

Celestine's awkwardness was palpable. A powerful man of the Spirit, he did not understand how to live and succeed among powerful men on earth. The values of the world were foreign to him.

The Pope and His Curia

The most dominant force in the late medieval Church was the practitioners of canon law. They were necessary to the growth of Christendom in the second half of the thirteenth century. The rise of powerful city-states, increased trade and communication between kingdoms, the transition from demonizing Eastern Christendom and Islam to attempting to understand them, and the burgeoning of universities throughout Europe—all of these matters required specialists. The experts in canon law inhabited the papal curia. They ran Western Christendom by an elaborate system of researchers, advisors, lawyers, judges, and courts. Originally intended to be a representative sample of the universal Church, the curia had by the time of Celestine V become the religious counterpart to a massive royal court. One scholar has referred to the curia as "the new bureaucratic superpower" that emerged during this era, as the papacy and its machinery came to dominate both the spiritual and temporal landscape.[4] There was nothing to compare to its power in any of the royal houses of Europe. Every single pope of that era was a canon lawyer, except Celestine.

Dante in the *Divine Comedy* disparages the way in which the Church was ruled by these legal experts who were schooled in the ability to judge and adjudicate. In the *Paradiso,* he laments how the "decretals," or books of church laws, had captivated the officers of the Church to the great neglect of the Gospels ("Evangel") and the Church Fathers ("the mighty Doctors").

For this the Evangel and the mighty Doctors
Are derelict, and only the Decretals
So studied that it shows upon their margins.

On this are Pope and Cardinals intent;
Their meditations reach not Nazareth,
There where his pinions Gabriel unfolded.[5]

More obsessed with the details and "margins" of ecclesiastical laws than the life and teachings of Jesus, these canon lawyers were consigned by Dante to the most undesirable eternal resting places.

In Celestine's case, the curia took over where Charles II had left them room. The hermit pope's spiritual charisma was a mismatch for the worldly leadership required for such an intricate, multilayered bureaucracy. They quickly followed their own agenda, knowing that their leader would have trouble discerning what they were up to.

The Final Weeks

As every area of his papal responsibilities fell into disarray, Celestine no longer felt capable of being either a spiritual leader or a manager of papal affairs. The curia didn't know how to function under a leader who was seemingly so disinterested, and they began to resist doing what the newly appointed agents of Charles II were insisting upon. Celestine, for his part, was not unaware of the disappointment he was causing. But there was little by then that he could do about it. He began to be addled, or simply confused, by difficulties. His contemporaries remarked at how unsophisticated his speech seemed to be. He often spoke in Italian, having little ability in the Latin used in church affairs.

He was communicating less and less with everyone at Castle Nuovo. He avoided contact with the curia, even Charles, and retreated more and more, spending time with his spiritual brethren only. The cardinals were more worried than ever, and on simple matters of governance they began to insist on face-to-face meetings with their pope, who needed to make decisions whether he wanted to or not. At these meetings it became clear that Celestine was either afraid or confused "and could only stammer out halting statements."[6] As one sympathetic archbishop summarized it, "He gave dignities, prelacies, offices, against all custom, at anyone's suggestion and the dictates of his own untutored simplicity."[7]

For a man like Peter, so strong with emotion, opinion, and desire, these final weeks must have been intensely difficult. To become head of the Western Church one had to be political, and Celestine did not have a political bone in his body. One had to be seeking power and influence, and the evidence seems to be that although Peter enjoyed the influence he'd held as a spiritual leader, he had the desire but not the understanding to wield his power in the world. A strong man in spiritual and physical terms, he was weak in the eyes of those who were better schooled in the ways of court, diplomacy, and chancery.

In early December 1294, Celestine attempted to turn over most of his responsibilities to a team of three cardinals. It's not unusual for a pope to delegate certain aspects of his responsibilities; what is unusual is the extent to which it has been done.

Pope John Paul II, for instance, was often lax in governing the late-twentieth-century curia, often leaving the everyday running of the Vatican to a variety of deputies. Benedict XVI has also indicated that his gifts and primary roles as holy father lie in teaching and writing, not in administrative duties. He also leaves the running of many things to others. But Celestine V's plan was far more extreme; it essentially would have created three popes instead of one, his advisors immediately said. The idea was promptly and wisely rejected, largely on the strength of the arguments of Cardinal Matthew Orsini, one of the most experienced members of the Sacred College, and a cardinal who participated in a total of thirteen papal conclaves over a long career.[8]

In the midst of all this, there was at least one group of people who were still excited about Celestine's ascension: the Franciscan Spirituals. Nicholas IV had been the first Franciscan pope, but as a Conventual he had felt threatened by these zealots and ordered that all Franciscans accept the ownership of property in common and pursue learning and education—pursuits that were contrary to the ideals of the Spirituals. Celestine became their champion.

The Spirituals were the most sincere believers that the papacy of Celestine signaled the advent of Joachim of Fiore's long-expected era of the Spirit of God. Under the previous pope they had been hiding—fearing for their lives—in the Marches of Ancona and other remote places throughout Italy—but now they came into the sunlight trusting that they would be protected. Celestine felt deeply for their plight. The venerable hagiographer Alban Butler writes: "To the rigorist *Spirituali* movement he was a pope sent direct from Heaven." Celestine gave his papal blessing to the efforts of the traditionalists, many of whom he knew personally, honoring their desire to remain faithful to the saint of Assisi. He gave them permission to live in separated, small hermitages, similar to those that once surrounded Francis's Portiuncula, and to practice Francis's Rule free of any outside interpretations from the papacy or elsewhere.

He also appointed one of their friars from the Marches, Ugolino of Brunforte, as the new bishop of Teramo. Notably this decision would be overturned by Boniface VIII within days following Celestine's abdication. In a papal bull Boniface declared: "That which was previously stipulated as righteous we are now expunging." Celestine also elevated to cardinal Berard of Got, the archbishop of Lyon who had ascended Mount Morrone in July to bring Peter the news of his election as pope. And he appointed Charles II's son, Louis, the next archbishop of Lyon—and Louis was only a twenty-one-year old layman. To his credit, Louis appears not to have accepted the appointment. His only qualification was that his private tutor had been a Spiritual Franciscan. He was to go on to become a saint himself (Saint Louis of Toulouse) and knew better than to accept what he was not yet ready to attain.

True to form, Celestine continued to exercise his spiritual authority in ways that demonstrated no understanding—or at least little fear of consequences—in his relationships with the leaders of the world. He grafted the Spirituals to himself. He made one of the Orsini family, Cardinal Napoleon Orsini, their official protector and guide, and for a time the Spirituals became known as *Pauperes eremitæ Domini Celestine,* the Poor Hermits of Pope Celestine, in honor of their champion. They were ordered to dress and live as hermits, a decision welcomed by the Spirituals as long as they would be safe. This was Celestine's greatest accomplishment as well as his final blunder. In the months and years after his death, it was the Spirituals who would most ardently maintain the holiness of the angelic pope, and bemoan how the world had destroyed him.

PART IV
THE PASSION AND THE PITY, 1294–96

Peter of Morrone . . . great is your rank and your worthiness,

But the tempest around you is no less,

Why, then, within your mansion

do you sit, questionless?

—JACOPONE OF TODI
"Epistle to Pope Celestine V"

I, PETER CELESTINE,
AM GOING AWAY

One hundred and forty miles away from Naples, the inscription on the dome of St. Peter's Basilica is taken from chapter sixteen of the Gospel of Matthew. It reads: *Tu es Petrus, et super hanc petram aedificabo ecclesiam meam et tibi dabo claves regni caelorum.* This was Latin that Peter actually knew, for he'd committed to memory most of the Gospels. "You art Peter, and on this rock I will build my church, and I will give you the keys of the kingdom of heaven."

He also knew the words of Christ from the cross: *Consummatum est*—"It is finished." It was this last utterance that Peter would emulate, much to the shocking of the world.

On the ceiling of the nave of the Church of Saint Peter of Maiella in Naples a Baroque fresco depicts Pope Celestine V removing his papal tiara from his head and handing it to someone else. Six monks look on with resignation and a single cherubim offers what appears to be a halfhearted blessing; the pudgy angel lackadaisically leans on his left hip and raises his right hand.

Celestine had renounced the papacy. How did it come

to this? No pope ever before had resigned. There had been plenty of forced resignations by methods such as poison (John VIII, 872–82, and his successor, Adrian III, 884–85); strangulation (Stephen VI, 896–97, and Leo V, 903); and other sordid means (see the next chapter), but never a willful resignation.

After all of the problems that had been encountered over the weeks Peter had spent as holy father, Charles II began to shelter the pope less and less. The king was just as baffled as were others about what to do. How can we get this pope to become more engaged in the affairs of the Holy See, to direct the clergy of Rome, to motivate the missions abroad, to inspire the world with the charisma and spiritual leadership that his reputation had promised? Why doesn't he seem to care much about his duties? The hermit pope had retreated fully into his shell. He was living a self-imposed exile within the king's estate. By December 1, 1294, the papal curia and conferences were humming along without much expectation that they would see their holy leader. From the beginning it had been obvious that Celestine was unprepared for his office, but now he seemed unwilling to even try.

In his cell the pope was contemplating abdication. First he weighed the spiritual justifications. He remembered the teachings of Peter Damian that he'd carried with him since his teenage years in Faifula: personal sanctity is the only sure path to genuine reform.

Celestine knew the ways to holiness better than he understood the ways of the papacy. As he considered the unthinkable—leaving his office behind—he prepared for what he believed to be the mature step of a Christian mystic: to follow Jesus into great suffering. The most famous Christian of that century had identified with Jesus so completely as to be gifted with the world's first known stigmata, and now a pope would identify with Jesus to the point of entering into a deep understanding of his passion. To abdicate would be equivalent to admitting weakness and failure—at least to those in the "world," but not to Peter Morrone. He knew the greater good of suffering. For him, walking away meant becoming a witness to sanctity. Stepping down from the Holy See was, in his mind, similar to Christ's willingly accepting his heavenly Father's will. The hermit pope felt ready for what might come next.

Again the example of Peter Damian took on great significance for Celestine, because Damian had once abdicated episcopal responsibility. Made the cardinal-bishop of Ostia by Leo IX, Damian served for a time with his usual aggressiveness. But after a short while, he pleaded with the pope to relieve him of the responsibilities of his see, so that the good and earnest monk could return to his primarily contemplative life, and Leo's successor finally allowed Damian to resign.

Damian always seemed to feel pessimistic when he was engaged in church business, and this feeling carried over to his experience as a cardinal. He never felt that he could make changes or bring about any reform when he was clothed in the finer garments of ecclesiastical leadership. Celestine imbibed these teachings deeply.

The world appeared to Damian to be on the threshold of its final end, according to him in this letter written at the end of his life, soon after he had returned from a churchwide synod:

> The world . . . is daily deteriorating into such a worthless condition, that not only has each rank of secular and ecclesiastical society collapsed and

fallen from its [former] state, but even monastic
life, if I may put it so, has declined and lies pros-
trate, deprived of strength to climb to its accustomed goals of perfection. Decency has gone,
honesty disappeared, religious devotion has fallen
on bad times.[1]

Damian goes on to exhort his readers to practice a true
spiritual life, which is possible only apart from the world.
He makes it clear that he himself has given up on other
courses of action. "Now, in the contract we made with
our God, it was we undoubtedly who said that in following Christ we promised to renounce the world and everything for which it stands." If we don't, he says, quoting
the words of Jesus from chapter nine of Luke, "if we look
back, we shall promptly hear the terrible pronouncement
of a threatening God: 'No one who sets his hand to the
plow, and then keeps looking back, is fit for the kingdom
of God.'"[2]

Celestine knew that as pope his personal limitations
were hurting, rather than helping, the God that he adored.
His love for the Church persisted in the fire of his devotion
and piety, making it more poignantly clear that he was unable to do his work. One historian of that age, Ptolemy
of Lucca, a Dominican who had been a friend and spiritual counselor to Thomas Aquinas, even says that there
were cardinals in the Sacred College who told Celestine
to fear for his soul, so confusing and dangerous was his
papacy for people everywhere. Ptolemy said that Celestine
was so disengaged in his final days at Castle Nuovo that
he was signing blank bulls put in front of him—which the
unscrupulous would later fill in to suit their purposes. Perhaps Celestine began to fear for his salvation if he were to

remain in his lofty position. And he knew that the poor were blessed and the rich have difficulty entering heaven.

When Celestine let it be known that he was thinking of abdicating, Charles II immediately voiced his opposition. We can imagine that the king set to work behind the scenes as well, asking every cardinal under his sway what could be done to keep his pope in place. Charles had a lot to lose, much more, in fact, than Celestine. He had accomplished what no sovereign before him had. He had kept the Christ of this earth in his own rooms, closely guarded his comings and goings, monitored who might be permitted to visit and counsel with him, and put in positions of power many from his own relations and personal interests. He couldn't allow all these accomplishments to amount to nothing.

In those first days of December, word began to spread that the pope was considering stepping down. Celestine clearly no longer desired the position and was making those feelings known to anyone who was paying attention.

On December 6, the Feast of Saint Nicholas of Myra, outside of the papal residence Franciscan Spirituals and Celestine monks began to gather, having heard the rumors through leaks in the papal entourage and among the cardinals. They surrounded the castle and carried on demonstratively in intercessory prayer for both the pope and the future of Mother Church. Charles II was there. Some say that he organized the rally. Ptolemy of Lucca was also among the crowd that day, just as he had been a witness to Celestine's election in Perugia.

These were the very last days before the onset of winter, when cold rain falls in Naples. The people were dispirited, full of dread, some even terrified. What would happen if a pope left his holy office? Some, believing that God might become furious, were on their knees with their rosaries. Others said that such an act could bring on that long-awaited dread, the advent of the true antichrist. Texts from the book of Daniel were read out:

> Daniel said, "I saw in my vision by night, and behold, the four winds of heaven were stirring up the great sea. And four great beasts came up out of the sea. . . . The first was like a lion and had eagles' wings. Then as I looked its wings were plucked off, and it was lifted up from the ground and made to stand upon two feet like a man; and the mind of a man was given to it. And behold, another beast, a second one, like a bear. It was raised up on one side; it had three ribs in its mouth between its teeth; and it was told, 'Arise, devour much flesh!'"
> (Dn. 7:1–5)

Penitents emerged, battering themselves in the hopes that whatever punishment they dealt to their own bodies God would not desire to bestow on them. A quitting pope could become a humiliation for the Church. Or, worse, some believed that it was like spitting in the face of God.

How could a pope relinquish something so precious and divinely appointed as the very "keys of heaven"? The eighth-century pope Adrian I had stated the importance of the papal office as follows: "The Lord set him who bears the keys of the kingdom of heaven as chief over all and by him is he honored with this privilege, by which the keys of the kingdom of heaven are entrusted to him. He, therefore, that was preferred with so exalted an honor was thought worthy to confess that faith on which the Church of Christ is founded. . . . And that power of authority, which he received from the Lord God our Savior, he too bestowed and delivered by divine command to the pontiffs, his successors."[3] Would Celestine throw this away, like casting scraps to the dogs?

Nothing had yet happened, but the authorities began to devise a plan for the pope to step down. Uncertainty reigned in Naples and rippled throughout Christendom for eight full days.

The Lawyers Go to Work

Celestine wanted to go, but he needed the assistance of experts in order to make his case.

Every ruler is surrounded by lawyers, and popes are no exception. The origins of canon law come from the "canons" established by the original apostles at the Council of Jerusalem circa 50 c.e. Going even further back, canon law can be traced to the tradition of expertise in Jewish law in the days of Jesus' youth, and the Pharisees and other legal experts with whom Jesus often conversed, as is recorded in the Gospels. Some famous canon lawyers in recent history have been Pope Benedict XV (1914–22), who trained as a civil lawyer before he was ever ordained to the priesthood; and Pope Pius XII (1939–58), the holy father who reigned during the Holocaust. Just as legal experts advise presidents and prime ministers on how to interpret laws and treaties, church lawyers provide similar services for rulers who are bound by ecclesiastical laws and precedent.

Canon lawyers have been behind-the-scenes actors in many of the most crucial episodes in religious history. For instance, when King Henry VIII was attempting to divorce his first wife, Catherine of Aragon, in order to marry his second wife (and third, and fourth, etc.), he consulted with canon lawyers. They worked during the night for weeks in order to find precedent and justification for what Henry desired to do. Similarly, in December 1294 Cardinal Gaetani rapidly began to investigate how it might be possible to justify the abdication of a pope.

Faced with many opportunities, canonists had for centuries considered the possibility of removing a pope for reasons of gross heresy. Each time such a maneuver was considered, the lawyers concluded that even if a man seemed unworthy of the office, the office (the papacy) was higher than any man. In the end, it was decided that no man could properly judge that a pope should be removed from the office. But never before had canon lawyers considered a willing, self-enacted, removal.

What Celestine and Gaetani were considering is not that far removed from the events of our own time. Many may remember that John Paul II was rumored to be considering resignation for years as his Parkinson's symptoms grew worse before our eyes. The Italian press periodically reported that his health was hanging by a thread, or that he was enduring near suffocation, or that he couldn't breathe fully on his own, or that he was suffering from some other problem connected with his chronic malady. On one occasion the Vatican's secretary of state, Cardinal Angelo Sodano, was asked whether or not John Paul II would ever consider resigning. The cardinal's answer made headlines around the world:

> If there is a man who loves the Church more than
> anybody else, who is guided by the Holy Spirit, if
> there's a man who has marvelous wisdom, that's
> him. We must have faith in the Pope. He knows
> what to do.[4]

A pope simply does not resign, many said. Who, after all, is "above" a pope who can accept such a resignation?[5] And the same media who quoted Cardinal Sodano in February 2005 also pointed out that there was a notorious case of a previous pope who'd resigned in the late thirteenth century. There was one precedent.

But in 1294 there was no such precedent. A case had to be prepared. We no longer possess whatever briefs Gaetani prepared for the holy father, but the cause for abdication was clear. Gaetani wrote for the pope a decree stating that a papal resignation was both possible and acceptable under certain circumstances. First, it was acceptable on the very grounds that made it most shocking: if it was clearly the voluntary act of a man in charge of all of his faculties. Second, it would have to be enacted in a proper and orderly fashion. And third, it could be done if it was absolutely necessary. On this last point there was no question remaining. There was no other course to take. Eight years later, the French philosopher John of Paris would summarize these conditions this way:

> If, after his election to the papacy a pope should
> find himself or should be discovered to be totally
> inept or useless or if an impediment should arise,
> such as insanity or anything similar, he should re-
> quest to be relieved by the people or by the cardinals

who in such a case represent the whole clergy and
people, and he should, permission received or not,
cede his high place.[6]

So Celestine not only had a plan of what to do but had
laid the groundwork to do it. He would move forward,
trusting Gaetani's advice.

THE NEW ADVENT OF FRIAR PETER

The Announcement

On December 12 Celestine was resolved in his decision. And then on December 13, the Feast of Saint Lucy, he read a statement out to the cardinals who had assembled to hear news that was, by that time, already well leaked.

First, he ordered them, by holy obedience, not to interrupt him. Then he read:

> I, Celestine V, moved by valid reasons, that is, by humility, by desire for a better life, by a troubled conscience, troubles of body, a lack of knowledge, personal shortcomings, and so that I may then proceed to a life of greater humility, voluntarily and without compunction give up the papacy and renounce its position and dignity, burdens and honors, with full freedom. I now instruct the Sacred College of cardinals to elect and provide,

according to the canons, a shepherd for the Universal Church.[1]

He'd declared himself to be essentially *inutilis,* "useless."

With this written resignation Celestine gave three reasons for his leaving: his old age, his desire for asceticism, and a spiritual temperament that made him a poor pope. At the conclusion of his statement, Celestine stepped down from the papal throne from which he'd stood countless times. He removed his ring, tiara, and mantle, handing them to the men who had elected him.

Then he sat down on the floor.

Within a few hours, Peter stepped back into the dress of the simplest of friars—the grey habit of a Celestine hermit—and prepared to leave. As he departed, most certainly secreted away from the crowd waiting outside, he probably felt a mix of relief and fear. The sounds of the street probably terrified him: the hum and swarms of people, sailors, servants, soldiers, merchants, horses, the clamor of wagons on rough stone streets, their barreled cargo rattling on its way to early morning destinations. He wanted neither castle nor city.

The Immediate Aftermath

Word of Celestine's resignation spread immediately. Before he surrendered the papacy, he had told the cardinals that they were to hold a papal election for his replacement. And his replacement would, of course, be the same man who had befriended him and helped him to resign the papacy. In fact, one of our most thorough records of

Celestine's statement on December 13 comes from Cardinal Gaetani. He tells the story thirty-nine months later in one small part of his large collection of canonical rules and papal bulls, *Liber Sextus* ("Six Books"), using the royal "Us" and "Our" common in papal self-reference:

> Some curious people have been arguing about things that are not very appropriate, and seeking rashly, against the teaching of the Apostle, to know more than it is good to know. They have seemed, without much thought, to raise anxious doubts as to whether the Roman Pontiff, even when he recognizes himself incapable of ruling the Universal Church and of bearing the burden of the Supreme Pontificate, can validly renounce his office, its burden, and honor, as in the person of Pope Celestine V, Our predecessor, who while still presiding over the government of this Church, wished to cut off all the matter for hesitation on the subject, deliberated with his brothers, the cardinals of the Roman Church, of whom We were one, and with the concordant counsel and assent of Us and of them all, by apostolic authority established and decreed, that the Roman Pontiff may freely resign.

From those first moments as Peter prepared to walk away, it appeared that Gaetani's aid had been disingenuous. During the election in Perugia five months earlier, Gaetani was not an obvious candidate, but even before Celestine stepped down Gaetani seemed to be at the center of everything. For his part, Gaetani made known to the other cardinals the close feelings that he shared with

Celestine and how he'd been instrumental in helping the saintly man escape the responsibilities that he clearly couldn't handle. There is even a story, later released by Gaetani himself, that the crownless Celestine came to him and begged him to correct his many mistakes.[2]

The Flight into Egypt

The hermit left Castle Nuovo on Christmas Eve 1294 as a free man and began his journey home to the Abruzzi. The holy man was looking to the mountains where he, again, might remember who he was and how to live his sanctified life.

By now eighty-five, the former pope had to have been accompanied on his journey by others. Most likely a retinue of the papal curia, the very few who remained faithful to the father of the Celestines, journeyed with him. As he set out in the direction of his home, people began to seek him out along the way. Enthusiasts, clergy, and the curious began to form around him. Peter made his way from the alien places surrounding Naples to the familiar locations closer to his friends and followers and home. He must have felt like a freed animal.

We don't know exactly how long Peter's journey north and east lasted. It couldn't have been more than a month or two. He seems to have traveled as far as his beloved Mount Morrone, to his secluded cell of Onofrio. That's all that he wanted—to return to his eremitic life. There he knew what he could do. There he was adored and respected. But Peter didn't feel safe at Onofrio for very long.

The evening before Peter left, the ten-day waiting period was coming to an end and the College of Cardinals got ready to name the next pope. The gathering of twenty-two cardinals knew of Gaetani's influence, expertise, and fierce intellect. He was outside of most of the intrigue between the competing families and the issues that usually split a conclave; and in this case, the cardinals understood the desperate need that the people were feeling for direction and firm leadership. Gathered at Castle Nuovo under Charles II's watchful eye, the College spent only one day in conclave, beginning late on December 23. Late that evening on the first ballot they elected Matthew Orsini, who declined the honor. On the second balloting, as Peter was walking through Naples, Benedict Gaetani won the majority.

Charles II watched these proceedings closely. The French king had become so powerful that Cardinal Gaetani saw fit to secure his endorsement before his election by the cardinals was confirmed. Gaetani visited with Charles, telling him that they would jointly fight the interests of the Ghibellines, and that as pope he would do all he could to help Charles retake Sicily. The election result was then announced to the crowd outside.

Cardinal Gaetani took the name Pope Boniface VIII. He left Naples by January 1, 1295, and was crowned at St. Peter's Basilica in Rome on January 23. Afterward he immediately went to the Lateran Palace to take it for himself and his office. For the new pontiff from Anagni, born and raised in the Papal States, there would be no more Neapolitan nonsense.

Boniface VIII's First Days

It was important to Boniface to control the narrative. The story of his friendship with Celestine was repeated in various ways. Boniface portrayed himself as the wise counselor who aided the angelic pope, and would now fix his many mistakes. Scribes and manuscript illuminators, in their own ways, commented on the shift of power. One book, housed in the Vatican Libraries, shows an image of Celestine in miniature leaving his throne in a small procession followed by eight men and a young page holding an umbrella over their heads. In the picture Cardinal Gaetani is being crowned at center left while Celestine is walking off the page in the far center right. Six of the cardinals are either holding their right hands to their hearts, or making a gesture of blessing. A decade later Giotto would paint a fresco depicting *Boniface VIII Addressing the People of Rome*—his first act after taking the pallium. Nothing but a fragment of this work still exists, but a seventeenth-century watercolor hanging in Milan shows what Giotto's work depicted: Standing in red cape and tiara, speaking to a large crowd below, is the new Pope Boniface. Most improbably, Celestine stands on the dais, off to the side, witnessing his successor's first address to the people of Rome. An orderly line of succession, the painting aims to suggest. But that was impossible. Celestine was nowhere near Rome on that day.

With Celestine far away, Boniface sat in his court and quickly began to undo much of what his predecessor had done, and to do what Celestine had left undone. But Boniface was full of uncertainties and concerned for his own authority in the eyes of the people. Would they continue to address Celestine as "holy father"? What would they call him, now that he was no longer Celestine V? Worst of all, what if the previous pope were to come back, having changed his mind?

Boniface didn't like the idea that another man might compete with him for papal authority. Peter was still alive, even if he was wandering the woods like Nebuchadnezzar, and that meant Peter was a threat. Also stories that didn't emerge in formal documents until a few years later were already being whispered about in the loggia of the Lateran Palace. Had Cardinal Gaetani been conniving before Celestine V abdicated? Was he the one who actually wrote Celestine's letter of abdication? How long before Celestine abdicated did the cardinal have himself fitted for his papal robes? Many voices were giving these rumors growing credence.

One legend, begun even during Celestine's lifetime, has Gaetani devising a scheme to trick Celestine in a way that's worthy of a medieval thriller. While Celestine was still on the throne, Gaetani created a megaphone device that would connect to Celestine's Castle Nuovo sleeping quarters from an adjoining room. He employed a suitably angelic voice and sent whispering, reassuring "locutions" to the foolish pope, visiting him with "divine" encouragement to resign.

Boniface, wanting to put his own fears at ease, sent word to Peter asking for a meeting. Peter knew enough about power and how it corrupts to see that such a meeting was something he should avoid. He kept moving.

Although Peter was unable to read most of the language of ecclesiastical business, there were certain Latin sentences that were imbedded in his soul. A monk dreamed and cried in words like, *Deus in adjutorium meum intende!* "O God, come to my assistance!" He had prayed that psalm in the darkness and early morning light for half a century (Ps. 69:1). At moments of great stress, we reach for what comforts and sustains us. This return to his hermit life was a crucial turning point in Peter's life, and such words would have come easily. This would be his *via crucis,* and he knew it.

The Capture

Boniface was afraid that Celestine's sympathies for the Spiritual Franciscans might gain him more and more followers in the mountains. And, of course, it would make perfect sense for the people to recognize the authority of this man. Being savvy, or astute, or even paranoid, Boniface feared that the people might not accept the former pope's resignation as easily as the College of Cardinals had done.

He didn't like the news that Peter was making himself difficult to find. However it was that he was receiving updates on Peter's situation, Boniface soon employed agents to hunt Peter on foot through the woods of the Abruzzi. An eighty-five-year-old hermit isn't difficult to track, and an ex-pope doesn't exactly travel unobtrusively. The new pope's agents traveled from village to village, mountain to mountain, sniffing out the old hermit. Peter did not suspect the extent to which Boniface would go. He may have been warned along his journey to be swift and careful, to get home to his cave as quickly as possible, and to stay there. Or perhaps he didn't believe the rumors that he might not be safe even if he made his way toward the sea.

Nevertheless, Peter left Onofrio not long after arriving there, and headed for Apulia, preparing to flee across the Adriatic. He stayed away from the port cities of Bari and Ancona and Brindisi. He wasn't far from Apulia, on a remote part of the shore where the coast rises and falls, shelving sharply toward the water. But the waters were rough, like the river torrents that flowed into the sea in the early spring.

The sea was known to rage, and the water was always dangerous at that time of year; there were few safe places for ships large or small to put in. Peter had never crossed there before, but like every man in the Abruzzi he had heard stories of dangerous crossings, aborted attempts, sunken vessels just offshore, and sailors who had been lost at sea within sight of their destinations. He also knew the legends of the leviathan that lurked in the deep. The psalmists had spoken of the awesomeness of God's creation: "O Lord, how manifold are your works! . . . Yonder is the sea, great and wide, which teems with things innumerable, living things both small and great. There go the ships, and Leviathan which you formed to sport in it" (Ps. 104:24–26). On the Adriatic coast Peter waited, making preparations for a difficult crossing.

In the end, Boniface's men found Peter rather easily on the easternmost coast of Italy. The poor ex-pope was near the village of Vieste, on the tip of the Gargano peninsula, about to begin a sea voyage to Dalmatia (part of today's Croatia). It was the middle of the night and a violent storm was raging. If they'd successfully made it to sea, Peter and his party could have found sanctuary on any of the islands sitting just off the coast of Dalmatia, which were Venetian towns in the late thirteenth century. But instead, when he was found on May 10, 1295, Peter was, to use the Italian, *inzuppato,* literally "soaked in the soup."[3]

Peter was taken quietly, and certainly against his will, to Anagni, the hometown of the new pope, to Boniface's own home, where Peter was held for many days while his captors waited to learn what their next steps might be. Anagni is an ancient Roman city where Cicero had once had an estate, as did many medieval popes. It was the birthplace of Boniface VIII, and a statue of him can still be seen high on the south wall of the Cathedral of Santa Maria. Playwright Peter Barnes has the two popes meeting face-to-face in Castle Nuovo after the abdication, and Boniface saying to Celestine, "Your virtue is contagion which will destroy Mother Church."[4] But it seems more likely that such a conversation, if it ever took place, happened at Anagni, a place where Boniface felt completely in control.

But keeping the ex-pope at Anagni couldn't be a long-term solution. He needed to be moved somewhere else where he would go unnoticed and be soon forgotten. Word came from Boniface that Peter should be taken to nearby Castle Fumone and held captive there. Castle Fumone sat along the ancient Roman road Via Casilina, connecting the Holy City with Naples, in the area now known as the Campagnia. Today Castle Fumone is near the town of Ferentino, situated just off the A1, the primary highway connecting Rome with cities to the south, and forty-six miles southeast of the capital city.

Why a castle? Certainly, Boniface didn't imagine that Peter would call for knights and mercenaries to come to his aid. By this time Peter was absolutely guileless. Nevertheless, he was to be guarded by a garrison of thirty-six men. Castle Fumone was positioned at a key post along Roman trading routes dating back to the time before Christ. It is set high on a hill, surrounded by forests, along the river that connected Rome to the key center of Capua, and standing on its ramparts soldiers could see danger coming from far away. *Fumone* is an Italian word that resonates with the French and English *fumere* and *fume*. It means literally "big smoke." Once this hill was a site for smoke warnings, which were used in the event of the threat of invasion.

Many popes have used castles as prisons and places for detaining, torturing, and executing enemies and heretics. Castle Sant'Angelo in Rome, beside St. Peter's Basilica, is where Pope John XIV (983–84) came to his end. Pope Paul II (1464–71) would give the order for twenty humanist scholars to be tortured on the rack at Castle Sant'Angelo in 1468; and Pope Clement VIII (1592–1605) held the famous Renaissance mathematician Giordano Bruno there for six years before having him executed before a crowd in the nearby market square, Campo de Fiori. The popes of Avignon in the fourteenth century also used their papal castle prison often. For a century before Peter's imprisonment, and for a few centuries afterward, Castle Fumone was a place for imprisoning enemies. It was there, for instance, that the antipope Gregory VIII (d. 1137) was once held captive by Pope Calixtus II. The site is a tourist attraction today, rented out for gala dinners, weddings, and corporate lunches. But it was an inauspicious place to be brought to during the thirteenth century.

Knowing his predecessor well and his weaknesses well, Boniface knew that Peter was no threat, yet the new pope decided that Peter must be imprisoned for the rest of his life. Boniface wasn't about to risk his enemies deciding to liberate and reinstall his spiritual foil.

MURDERED BY A POPE

In the days of the Roman Empire, after Christianity was
established as the religion of state, the Church established
prisons for detaining ecclesiastical officials who were seen
as having begun to err in their ways and needed some cor-
rection. The idea was to create secure places where one
dissenter would not influence others, and so that there
might not be any shedding of blood.[1]

Celestine's captivity was just this sort of custody and
exile, rather than punishment or rehabilitation. What
could he have been charged with, other than perhaps
disturbing the peace? Late medieval sentences often included public shaming, forced amputations, payment of
debts and fines, the confiscation of property, imprisonment, and exile. Something in between the two latter options seems to have been intended for the ex-pope. He was
simply going to be held.

Peter's imprisonment at Fumone wasn't the first in
which Boniface VIII had been involved. In 1281, during
the conclave that elected the French pope Martin IV, the

papal legate Gaetani played a part in the brief imprisonment of his opponent Cardinal Matthew Orsini "in squa-
lor, with scant bread and little water, even to the damage of
his constitution."[2] They played rough in those days. Soon
after, Martin IV elevated Gaetani to cardinal and put a red
hat on his head.[3]

We have no direct evidence that conditions were harsh
for Peter at the castle. It's worth considering that his
situation was probably no worse than what he would have
willingly chosen for himself and his fellow hermits in the
Abruzzi.[4] But this is to ignore the difference between living in voluntary poverty and living at the mercy of another.
Peter Morrone had always reveled in access to open air and
free spaces. A castle prison was something else entirely.

The old man had left Naples with such hope and op-
timism in his heart. "He seemed to withdraw easily, his
shoulders removed from a yoke, his neck from a fatal
axe," wrote the poet Petrarch. And now it had come to
this. Within the span of less than a year, Peter had been a
renowned hermit, a failed pope, and a wandering hermit,
and finally finished up wasting away in prison.

But, Murder?

The suggestion that he was murdered is not far-fetched.
By varying accounts there have been as many as twenty
popes who were murdered over the course of history. As
many as "a third of the popes elected between 872 and
1012 [alone] died in suspicious circumstances," according
to Eamon Duffy.[5] The list of those who have been killed
looks something like this:

- John VIII (872–82) was likely poisoned and then beaten and left for dead.
- Adrian III (884–85), his successor, was also poisoned.
- Stephen VI (896–97) was thrown into prison and strangled by his political enemies.
- Leo V (903) seems to have been strangled by the pontiff who succeeded him.
- John X (914–28), a vigorous, warring man, was suffocated in his sleep by the young mistress of the future Pope Sergius III.
- Stephen VII (929–31) was most likely murdered.
- Stephen VIII (939–42) was "horribly mutilated," in Duffy's words.[6]
- John XII (955–64) became pope at the age of seventeen and was a warring pope and one of the most completely corrupt popes in history. He seems to have been murdered by the jealous husband of one of the women he'd been sleeping with.
- Benedict VI (973–74) was either poisoned or strangled on the orders of some Roman politicians.
- John XIV (983–84), like our man Celestine V, died either by starvation or murderous neglect, while imprisoned in Rome at Castle Sant'Angelo by his political and religious enemies.
- Gregory V (996–99), the first German pope, died so suddenly and amid so much contention that poison is suspected.
- Sergius IV (1009–12) was likewise poisoned.
- Clement II (1046–47) was either poisoned with lead sugar, or he took lead that was intended for medicinal purposes and was poisoned.

- Damasus II (1048), Clement II's successor, was such an awful pope that since we don't know why he died, we assume that he, too, was probably murdered.
- Celestine V (1296–?)
- Benedict XI (1303–4), who succeeded Boniface VIII, died so suddenly and seemingly without cause that again foul play is suspected. John Cornwell names the cause "powdered glass in his figs."[7]
- Even in our own lifetime John Paul I (1978), who canceled his own coronation ceremony for simplicity's sake and was often accused of "naivete and ignorance of world affairs,"[8] died just thirty-three days after his election. He was only sixty-five years old and was found sitting up in bed. The official cause of death was given to the world as a heart attack suffered during the night. But without an autopsy (forbidden on a pontiff), and given the rapid embalming (also customary), as well as a vow of silence (imposed on all who were present that morning), poison has seemed plausible to both historians and conspiracy theorists.[9]

In addition, there have been other popes who have been plotted against without success. The Avignon pope John XXII (1316–34) was nearly poisoned to death by a cadre of accomplices of the bishop of Cahors. John XXII, who from the moment he became pope lived extravagantly, had accused the bishop of simony and other abuses of power; the bishop, in turn, plotted to poison John, using magic and arsenic in his bread, so as to do the deed undetected. The bishop was found out and John declared that "legally, a murder by poison was worse than one committed with a sword"; he stripped the bishop of his clerical status, dragged him through the city streets, and then burned him at the stake.[10]

There's a precedent for both murderous and murdered popes.

God's representative on earth isn't always safe. Still, it is interesting that although the secular rulers of the Middle Ages often behaved in ways that showed that they had no respect for a religious man, they nevertheless considered the Holy See in a privileged position, such that they rarely felt emboldened to simply strike down a pope. Any killing had to be done deftly, secretively, carefully. Their usurping or vengeful or simply retaliatory motivations had to be disguised. Perhaps even their own souls demanded coups that had some semblance of a spiritual solution, as well. Today we would call this perception over reality: a pope with a knife in his back has been murdered, but a poisoned pope may have been called home by the Almighty.

One of the most common iconographical images of Celestine V depicts the hermit holding a palm branch, the symbol of a martyr's death. But if he died accidentally or of natural causes while in that castle, why would his death be considered a martyrdom? This question has never been answered. Speculation was rampant even in the summer of 1296.

In the Castle Darkness

There is of course no physical evidence of what happened to Peter, nor are there any firsthand accounts from prison guards. A century later Biondo Flavio of Forli (1392–1463), a humanist scholar and civil servant, a secretary to princes, and member of the papal curia in Rome, left us something. As an elderly man, having served four popes, Biondo was a true insider in the early Renaissance curia when people were still interested in trying to figure out what had happened to Peter Morrone. In his classic period work, *Italy Illuminated,* Biondo devotes only one manuscript page to summarizing the events surrounding Peter's death, but he records an idea that had begun circulating soon after Peter's death:

> [Boniface] had compelled Celestine V—a simple soul and a saintly man who had honored Boniface with the papacy that he himself resigned—to die in prison at Fumone.[11]

Is this true? And if so, how might it have happened?

A number of theories have been put forward over the centuries. For example, we know that he was not strangled. He was not stabbed. He was not starved to death. He did not die of a stroke or a heart attack. All of these causes of death would have left physical manifestations on the body that would have been understood even by late-thirteenth-century physicians. Many people saw Celestine's dead body and none spoke of any signs to indicate he died in any of these ways.

Whatever happened it was more subtle than that.

So, then, perhaps he died of old age. He was eighty-five, after all—well beyond the average lifespan of a man of his era. A death resulting from old age was the official cause given. An old, revered ex-pope had died while residing near the childhood home of his successor.

But Peter had languished at the Fumone castle for ten

straight months. He died on May 19, 1296. And it appeared to those who saw the body that he may have been suffering from what looked like an infection from an untreated wound to the skin. This suggests severe treatment, or at least negligence. Was Peter abused? What did Boniface know, do, or not do? Another theory is that the ex-pope was murdered by his successor.

The Nail in the Head Theory

A fascinating, possible scenario emerged in the earliest days after Celestine's death. Imagine Boniface himself going to the castle to see Celestine. Quietly and secretly. Perhaps he approached the older man's cell to ask for his forgiveness. What a fascinating scene that would have been: the saintly hermit expecting the best of the conniving Boniface, the old man looking to the younger man for respect. Without any attendants or members of the curia or even an attendant or prison guard present, Boniface could have visited Peter's cell (prison cell, not monastic cell) and repented his sins. Who else might a pope confess to but another pope?

And what might those sins have been? Greed, connivance, slander—all in the service of achieving his goal of ascending to the chair of St. Peter. Boniface may have been culpable for forcing Celestine's abdication, or even for stealing his office. We will never know for certain what happened.

In August of 1998 an Italian monk, Reverend Quirino Salomone, caused international headlines when he produced a theory that Celestine's death may have been

214 The Pope Who Quit

caused by a nail driven into the side of his head. Salomone claimed to have discovered a half-inch hole in Celestine's left temple by means of a CAT scan.[12] But there is nothing conclusive in Salomone's "discovery." In fact, scholars have long known about the hole in his skull. One historian wrote eighty years ago: "The corpse [of Celestine V] was seen by many, and bore no trace of foul play. Today his skull, treasured at L'Aquila, has a nail-hole in the temple, but beyond question it is of later manufacture."[13] All of this begs the question: whose remains do we possess, and which remains were examined eighty years ago, or more recently? We'll never know exactly whose skull it is and how it came to have a hole in it.

The Poisoning Theory

How, then, did Celestine die?

The evidence seems to point to at least one thing for certain: Boniface had no intention of allowing Celestine to live freely. He locked him up for life, knowing that the old man wouldn't live much longer. But we have no physical evidence of the cause of death. There is no corpse, and there were no direct eyewitness accounts and no autopsy.

Nevertheless, the Middle Ages was a time of scientific discovery. The works of Hippocrates and Galen were translated into Arabic in the eighth century as physicians in the East rediscovered the power of medicines. A few centuries later, the work of these pioneering Muslim thinkers made its way West. The ancient theory that the human body was composed of four humors (black bile, yellow bile, phlegm, and blood) was finally discredited,

researches were undertaken to comprehend human anat-
omy, and surgeries were once again practiced. Renewed
forms of medical knowledge were born in the late Middle
Ages and so was knowledge about the potency and accu-
racy of poisons, building upon the work done long before
by the ancient Mesopotamians, Egyptians, and Greeks.
Ancient theories gave way during the twelfth and thirteenth centuries to true developments in the use of
herbs and chemicals to both heal and harm. In certain
times and places these were commonly used by experienced and confident practitioners. The medicinal use of
herbs (such as lavender, nightshade, hemlock) wasn't limited to physicians, but in fact was most common among
professions such as dentists, midwives, and monastic gar-
deners. There was also a flourishing trade in herbs used
for more magical purposes. The annals are full of stories
of women using concoctions to induce their husbands to
love them, or other "old wives" tales and charms.

Poisoning matches the subtlety required to end the life
of a prominent religious rival. After Celestine had been
kept in that prison for several months, those who guarded
him might have been surprised that the elderly man had
not yet died of natural causes. Perhaps they concocted another plan.

Since ancient Babylonia, we have evidence of the use
of real poisons, as well as antidotes to poison.[14] Ancient
philosophers such as Galen spoke often of poisons. The
first-century Roman historian Tacitus wrote about rumors
that the emperor Nero had poisoned one of his enemies
under the ruse of healing him from his ailments.[15] Queen
Cleopatra is said to have compiled a book of poisons acute
to the sense of sight (to glimpse them was to fall under
their spell). Many naturally occurring plants and other

natural substances were understood to be toxic and dangerous to humans. At the same time, in nearly every ancient civilization simple antidotes such as vinegar were used to counteract some of the effects of poisonous substances, including snakebites. Human beings have understood that certain animals, vegetables, and minerals are dangerous ever since the Garden of Eden; and they have known how to use salves of various kinds for just as long.

Nearly every field of knowledge benefited from the work of Islamic scholars. Through the transmission of various Arabic texts and their translation into Latin, Western physicians and students followed the advances coming from the East. Many famous Western religious figures wrote small tracts on poisons, stimulated by these new researches. The preeminent Jewish philosopher Maimonides (1135–1204) was one, and the scholastic theologian Robert Grosseteste (ca. 1170–1253) was another. The following definition of a poison, as stated in one medieval Arabic text, fairly represents the understanding of the era:

> A poison . . . is overpowering in its nature. . . . It is
> not an accident but it exists permanently. Poison
> is something which overpowers and destroys that
> which is called the life force of an animal. When it
> overcomes this force, the functioning of the organs
> of the body is disturbed. The liver, stomach, and
> veins cannot function so that the strength of the
> heart, liver, brain, arteries, warmth, and sinews cannot be transported through the body as they were
> previously. The quality of this condition is the characteristic of death since, in consequence of these
> things, it corrupts the breath which gives rest to
> the body.[16]

Much of the work on poisons remained superstitious, full of myth and magic, such as ideas about poisonous sights and sounds; nevertheless, the following areas became more sophisticated in the decades leading up to the late 1290s:

- Treatments of snake, rat, and scorpion bites.
- Ways of keeping food safe from poisonous substances.
- Diagnosing symptoms related to the ingesting of poison.

And dozens of poisonous concoctions were known to exist, their recipes orally transmitted as well as physically circulated in the libraries of Europe. These included animal (frogs, spiders, lizards, animal blood, tarantula, bats), vegetable (coriander, fleawort, toadstool), and mineral (arsenic, mercury, vitriol) ingredients.

The symptoms of poison were well known as well. Someone who ate or drank poison was known to lose color, show confusion of mind, tremble, perspire, laugh, become languid, or become frightened. There were books of symptoms, therapies, and cures for the one who came upon a poisoned person without having seen the cause of the ailment. It was common to attempt to force vomiting, but if that didn't work, various herbs and minerals were prescribed.

One of the questions surrounding Boniface and Celestine is this: Did the younger pope poison the elder? Boniface certainly had motive, opportunity, and means.

218 The Pope Who Quit

Motivations for Murder

The first textual evidence we possess for hypothesizing that Celestine was murdered by Boniface comes from documents written by Boniface's opponents, so they cannot be absolutely trusted. In early May 1297 formal accusations were first made against Boniface; he was called "the illegitimate usurper" of the chair of Peter and accused of having used undue and deceptive influence over Celestine. And at least by March 1303 Boniface was accused of being complicit in his predecessor's death.

On May 10, 1297 (two years to the day after Peter was captured by Boniface's men on the Adriatic coast), Cardinals James and Peter Colonna wrote the following to the canon law experts at the University of Paris:

> By evil advice and false arguments he and his accomplices persuaded our lord pope Celestine V of happy memory to renounce the apostolic office, though this was contrary to the rules and statutes of divine, human and canon law and a cause of scandal and error to the whole world. Then, when Celestine had resigned the papacy *de facto*—for he could not do so *de iure* since it is clear to all who are willing to investigate the matter carefully that the Roman pope cannot resign or give up the papacy or be released from it except by God alone—he did not fear to put himself *de facto* since he could not do it *de iure* in the place of the same lord Celestine.[17]

These accusations were published far and wide, spreading the conspiracy theory rapidly throughout Italy. It was said that "during the day, the manifesto was fixed on the doors of several churches in Rome and even laid on the high altar of St. Peter's."[18]

The Colonna brothers were essentially fighting with Pope Boniface over property and power; for all practical purposes, James and Peter were at war with Boniface. The surrounding curia and cardinals knew as much. This was partisan politics full of self-interest on both sides. Nevertheless, the arguments of the Colonnas were also considered on the merits, and since they reflected the feelings of a growing number of people both inside the Roman curia and out, people believed them. Franciscan poet Jacopone of Todi took to referring to Boniface as a "new Lucifer . . . on the papal throne" at about this same time. Many clergy, including bishops residing outside of Italy, signed the Colonna manifesto.

Meanwhile, one of the leaders of the Spirituals, Peter Olivi, a theologian of great renown who died at the age of fifty in 1298, weighed in on the matter. The year before his death he came to the defense of both popes, saying that Celestine's resignation was justified. In response to the Colonnas' letter, Olivi distinguished between the sacramental office of the holy father (handed down from Saint Peter) and the juridical office of the pope. The first can never be removed, while the second, can, Olivi said. A bishop has always been able to remove the juridical function from another priest, he argued, and the bishop of Rome has always been able to do the same with another bishop under his direction. "By arguing that the pope has the same authority over himself as he has over other bishops, Olivi even went further and claimed for him not only the right to resign . . . but to nominate his own successor as well."[19] The Spirituals, who were his followers, called Peter Olivi a saint; and the Conventuals, who ruled the order, would eventually call him a heretic and a generation later would desecrate his grave.

The Colonnas' charges were repeated a variety of times and in a number of places over the next decade. One scholar has summarized what happened this way: "The abdication of Pope Celestine V was interpreted, especially by the adversaries of his successor . . . as an uncanonical 'divorce' from the universal Church to which the pope was married."[20] We have this reflection from 1303 by the French theologian William of Plaisians, which shows how the Colonnas' ideas had deepened in the six years since they were first published. In a long list of heresy charges brought against Boniface VIII, this is the twenty-sixth:

> It is notorious that he [Boniface VIII] treated his predecessor Celestine inhumanely, a man of holy memory who led a holy life; and that, because Celestine could not resign and because, therefore, Boniface could not legitimately succeed to the Holy See, the latter threw him in prison and had him quickly and secretly killed. And all this is widely and publicly known by the whole world.[21]

Soon Jacopone of Todi coined this prophecy about Boniface VIII: "You crept into the papacy like a fox, you will reign like a lion, and you will die like a dog." And sure enough, Boniface was nearly killed by his enemies. On September 7, 1303, he was abducted at his home in Anagni by one of the Colonnas together with William of Nogaret, whom Boniface had also excommunicated for calling him a criminal. The two men beat him for three days, leaving him humiliated but still pope. Boniface died a month later.

A century later the Renaissance humanist Biondo Flavio recorded that Boniface came to his own bad end because he was complicit in the death of Celestine. Meanwhile, the *Catholic Encyclopedia* considers it a calumny to state "that Boniface treated him [Celestine] harshly, and finally cruelly murdered him." We'll never know for certain, but in the end Celestine died while held captive by Boniface. And there are no reasons why the new pope would have wished for the papa angelico to live.

19

THE WORLD IS FALLING APART

Sociologist Émile Durkheim once wrote: "When a society is going through circumstances which sadden, perplex, or irritate it, it exercises a pressure over its members, to make them bear witness, by significant acts, to their sorrow, perplexity, or anger. It imposes upon them the duty of weeping, groaning or inflicting wounds upon themselves or others . . . restor[ing] to the group the energy which circumstances threaten to take away from it."[1]

After Peter's passion, the disciplinati came back stronger than ever before. Throughout the opening years of the new century, during the pontificate of Boniface the usurper, these penitents grew in number all over Italy and Europe. Within half a generation, led by another enigmatic monk, Venturino of Bergamo, a group of more than 10,000 men and women with whips made its way to the steps of St. Peter's in Rome during Lent 1335. They marched for peace and repentance. They desperately wanted to make an appeal to the thrones of power but also to people everywhere. But they would be frustrated. By then the pope was in Avignon, France.

Within three days of his election, Boniface VIII had rescinded every favor of leniency that Celestine had granted. Many of the Franciscan Spirituals fled to faraway places such as Greece and Sicily to "withdraw from the brothers' wrath and . . . that they should retreat to . . . freely serve the Lord," according to Angelo Clareno, who took over their leadership in 1305 and wrote the history of the period.[2] Jacopone of Todi, the Spirituals' poet, wrote searing verses about churches weeping, souls floundering, and true virtue wasting away. "No Earthly stuff / Deserves your heart's desire," he laments to his brothers.

> *You are not nourished by created things*
> *Your body's wings [the soul]*
> *To other realms must fly.*[3]

Their hope had vanished. There didn't even seem to be reasons left for living on this earth; they should, the poet counseled, live only in "heaven."

The Spirituals, who were by then one with the order of Celestine hermits, had rejected Boniface VIII as their holy father and were promptly (and understandably) excommunicated by him. One might imagine that the order slid into oblivion after these events, but it didn't. In fact, 250 years later they had some ninety monasteries, including ones near Paris, as well as in Barcelona and Bohemia.[4] They lasted until the Napoleonic era.

In the Kingdom of Naples and beyond it seemed that darkness had settled over everything. The people slowly heard the stories of what had happened, that Celestine was dead, and their loss of hope was reflected, they believed, in floods, searing heat waves, and winter storms.

Mystical experience became more pronounced and prominent in religious life. What started as a single experience of stigmata by Francis of Assisi eighty years earlier became a near-commonplace claim of women and men throughout Western Europe in the early decades after Celestine's death. Meanwhile, acts of personal asceticism became more popular than ever, as people's apocalyptic fears rose to extraordinary levels.

Epidemics flared, and again people saw God's hand in the dangers and in their losses. There were various outbreaks of bubonic plague leading up to the Black Death pandemic that took place from 1348 to 1350, during which half the population of Europe died, more than thirty million people. The feeling of impending death was in every café, village square, and church. Boccaccio cynically wrote that men were having lunch with their friends at home and then dinner with their ancestors in the afterlife. The most popular hymn of the fourteenth century was penned by Thomas of Celano, Saint Francis's first biographer. It was called *Dies irae* or "Day of Wrath," and the opening lines read like this:

> *Day of wrath, O day of mourning!*
> *See fulfilled the prophet's warning,*
> *Heaven and earth in ashes burning.*
> *Oh, what fear man's bosom rendeth*
> *When from Heav'n the Judge descendeth*
> *On whose sentence all dependeth!*[5]

Jacopone of Todi wrote verses about such things as well, contemplating the meaning of impending physical death in one his most famous works, *Laude*. The poem imagines the world as an awful place where human desire is always foiled ultimately by God. There are images of bare skulls shorn of their flowing hair, once bright eyes gone from their sockets, "the worms have gnawed them, and have quenched their light," and a tongue that may have been cut out, or perhaps "your teeth have gnawed it off corrosively!" The concluding quatrain goes like this:

> *Now look on me, O man of worldly mind;*
> *No longer in this world will you pleasures find;*
> *For step by step, I think you are foolish and blind!*
> *You'll be bound and shackled most cruelly!*[6]

These were more than omens; they were presages of a new age, a time when the end of one era was being marked and an ominous vision was being expressed about the era to come. Angelo Clareno claimed that this was all God's will and judgment. As he eerily put it, the people of the early fourteenth century were living in the midst of a tribulation period that was the consequence of Pope Celestine's abdication, and had been foretold before he was elected: "A certain person is said to have received from an angel of the Lord before the election of Lord Celestine, namely that for twenty-eight years after his renunciation a great tribulation would take place."[7] It would be a century before the Renaissance would flood any real illumination into these darkest of times.

The French cardinal and theologian Pierre d'Ailly wrote a Life of Celestine V in 1407. He echoed Angelo Clareno's interpretation of events and lay responsibility for the divisions in the Church at the feet of Boniface VIII: "[Celestine V's] example of honorable humility should have been imitated by those who, in these times of misery and suffering, have done all they could to attain this supreme honor. Then the Church would not have been riven for thirty years by their horrible discord and disastrous schism."[8]

In many respects the Middle Ages came to an end right about the time when the hermit pope died in a castle prison.

Celestine V was the latest, and for many, the last, hope of those who believed that a man could wield both political and spiritual power and rule the one apostolic Church and the world with the wisdom of King Solomon and the compassion of Christ. To those who saw the calamities of the 1300s as God's judgment, Peter Morrone's papacy represented a failed attempt to raise a profoundly spiritual, unworldly man to the throne in the expectation that the world would follow him. Just as some of Christ's disciples were disappointed that he didn't come to earth to be a temporal ruler, those in power crushed Celestine when they saw his glaring political and social incapacities.

The Middle Ages have been called many things, including "when Europe was 'Christendom'" by Paul Johnson.[9] The period that saw the burgeoning of monasticism, mystical and subtle thinkers such as Pseudo-Dionysius and Thomas Aquinas, and the building of soaring Gothic cathedrals was a period when most people believed that religion would sort and solve life's problems and give life meaning. Christendom, for good and for bad, flourished, dominating every aspect of life. With the episode of Celestine V, the dissolution of the Church's influence over the State took one step closer to becoming reality.

For centuries people had believed that a pope was chosen by the guiding hand of God, and his success, despite any possible corruption or problems, was entirely in God's will. Similarly, every king and queen and prince was believed to rule by divine authority. There were no truly secular rulers; princes and lords functioned almost like clergy in their responsibilities for the welfare of the people under their power. No longer. Since the turn of the fourteenth century, we have lived in the era of cynicism toward both religious and civil authority. There is no acceptance that their interests are our interests.

The papa angelico experiment was a clear failure. The effects were felt everywhere.

Consolidation of Power

As much as Boniface VIII is remembered for his relations with his predecessor, he is just as notable for his bull on papal supremacy. This was the papacy's greatest temporal power grab yet. On November 18, 1302, Boniface issued *Unam Sanctam* (Latin for "The One Holy"), which charted a decisive course for how the Church relates to the world. For the first time it was made doctrine that salvation was impossible outside of the sacraments of the Roman Catholic Church. Boniface employed a variety of metaphors and references to Scripture in order to make this point. Perhaps most powerfully, he compared the singularity of the Church to the ark of Noah: "It was finished in one cubit and had one helmsman and captain, namely Noah, and we read that all things on Earth outside of it were destroyed."[10] Perhaps the most famous papal bull ever written by any pope in history, *Unam Sanctam* states:

> Therefore, if the Earthly power errs, it shall be judged by the spiritual power, if a lesser spiritual power errs it shall be judged by its superior, but if the supreme spiritual power errs it can be judged only by God not by man, as the apostle witnesses, "The spiritual man judgeth all things and he himself is judged of no man" [1 Cor. 2:15]. Although this authority was given to a man and is exercised by a man it is not human but rather divine, being given to Peter at God's mouth, and confirmed to him and to his successors in him, the rock whom the Lord acknowledged when he said to Peter himself "Whatsoever thou shalt bind" etc. [Mt. 16:19]. Whoever therefore resists this power so ordained by God resists the ordinance of God.[11]

This successor to the saintly pope was attempting to solidify the temporal power of the papacy, over and above all other earthly rulers. The angelic course of action had failed miserably; now it would be demonstrated that the only spiritual qualification necessary for world rule was an election to the chair of Peter.

Boniface's position was made easier by the works of a theologian written 150 years earlier. In 1150 the Cistercian abbot Bernard of Clairvaux wrote a famous letter to his friend and former pupil Pope Eugenius III. The Second Crusade had recently and disastrously failed, and the occasion of Bernard's letter was to urge Eugenius to wield the full power of the Church, which had been diminished by weakness and corruption, to call another crusade to the Holy Land. In the process, Bernard articulated what quickly came to be known as the "two swords theory" of how secular power derives entirely from Church and pope. The argument goes like this: Both swords are held by the Church, and the princes who rule the temporal world use their sword only at her request or for her benefit.

There are "spiritual and temporal swords," Bernard wrote, "and the second one is to be drawn *for* the Church, while the first one is drawn *by* the Church."

Bernard compared these swords to the one that Saint Peter carried on the night of Christ's arrest outside the Garden of Gethsemane. Remember: Peter famously lashed out to protect Jesus, cutting off the right ear of the high priest's servant. When Jesus told Peter to stop acting so rashly, it was essentially the Lord and Savior commanding the first pope to put his sword back into its sheath (see Jn. 18:11)—even if just for a time. In 1150 Bernard was urging his friend, saying that it was now time for the Church to take both swords out.[12] Pope Eugenius III appreciated such an argument. Why wouldn't he? It would be rare for a person in power to argue that he should *not* exercise the power that is granted to him.

Another predecessor of Boniface VIII, Pope Innocent III, then built on Bernard of Clairvaux's theory and consolidated papal power by extending it to cover every human being on the planet. It didn't matter that not every human being was Christian or resided within Christendom; the pope was the vicar of Christ for the entire earth. Each duly elected man sat in Christ's stead. This is how Innocent III put it, when he not so graciously accepted the submission of King John of England (sealer of the Magna Carta and the king of Robin Hood legends) to papal authority in 1214:

> Jesus Christ . . . has so established in the Church His kingdom and His priesthood that the one is a kingdom of priests and the other a royal priesthood, as is testified by Moses in the Law and by Peter in his Epistle; and over all He has set one whom He has appointed as His Vicar on Earth, so that, as every knee is bowed to Jesus, of things in heaven, and things in Earth, and things under the Earth, so all men should obey His Vicar and strive that there may be one fold and one shepherd. All secular kings for the sake of God so venerate this Vicar, that unless they seek to serve him devotedly they doubt if they are reigning properly.[13]

All created life was subject to the pope. And the pope was in turn subject to no one but Christ.

These notions endured into the thirteenth century. When Peter was a young leader of hermits on Mount Morrone, Innocent IV (1243–54) also took up Bernard of Clairvaux's metaphor and instructed the use of the temporal sword in all manner of ways, showing that there was no distinction between the spiritual and temporal realms of his authority. He appointed an administrator of Portugal, granting kingdoms to princes just as emperors might do. He took sides with King Henry III of England, contrary to the wishes of the bishops of that land. He even sent ambassadors to the Muslim Mongols, telling them that as Christ's vicar it was within his power to punish them if they continued to break the Ten Commandments.

Exercising power often turned into abusing power. In 1282, for example, only a dozen years before Celestine V was elected, Pope Martin IV excommunicated the entire island of Sicily as punishment for their revolt. Today a single papal excommunication can make headlines around the world, and the reasons are examined and debated on all sides. Imagine today: The pope excommunicates the inhabitants of . . . Scotland! But in the Middle Ages a pope was much more than a spiritual figure. He was more than a man with political influence. He was more than a king. He was, in effect, God on earth. It was a position that Boniface relished.

With *Unam Sanctum* Boniface argued that both the spiritual and temporal swords were in his power. Expanding on the famous analogy of Bernard of Clairvaux, Boniface wrote: "[T]he one is exercised for the church, the other by the church, the one by the hand of the priest, the other by the hand of kings and soldiers, though at the will and suffrance of the priest. One sword ought to be under the other and the temporal authority subject to the spiritual power."[14]

Within a few years of the death of Boniface VIII in 1303, the city of Rome was being lamented as the capital of an empire that once was, and the papacy was in retreat to the South of France. Pope Benedict XI then ruled for less than a year, dying in 1304, most likely murdered. Pope Clement V was elected in 1305 and in 1309 began what is known as the Avignon papacy. After this Frenchman fled

Italy for the next sixty-seven years popes were dominated by French politicians and noblemen, ruling entirely from Avignon. Seven consecutive popes ruled from southern France rather than from Rome:

- Clement V, 1305–14 (Raymond Bertrand of Got)
- John XXII, 1316–34 (Jacques d'Euse)
- Benedict XII, 1334–42 (Jacques Fournier)
- Clement VI, 1342–52 (Pierre Roger)
- Innocent VI, 1352–62 (Etienne Aubert)
- Urban V, 1362–70 (Guillaume Grimoard)
- Gregory XI, 1370–78 (Pierre Roger of Beaufort)

The last French pope in history to be recognized by the Church (there were antipopes after this), was Gregory XI, who died on March 27, 1378.

Following on the heels of the Avignon papacy was the Great Papal Schism of 1378–1415, when at least two men at once claimed to be pope, further undermining the prospects for a consolidated Church with temporal or spiritual authority. Birgitta Gudmarsson, the famous and wealthy widow with eight children who founded a religious order and experienced visions of Christ, known to history as Saint Bridget of Sweden, tells us a lot about what happened during these exile years. She was in Rome doing penance for the failures of Christendom, urging anyone who would listen that the pope must come home. The Church was in ruin and in need of saving. Throughout her *Liber Celestis* (Book of Heaven) Bridget laments like a Hebrew prophet the lost glory of the city of Rome:

> I see with my own eyes that there are many churches
> where the bodies of blessed saints lie in rest. Some of

these buildings have been enlarged, but the hearts of the men who administer them are away from God.

Rome, Rome, your walls are broken and your gates are unguarded! Your sacred vessels have been sold and your wine, sacrifices, and incense have all been wasted. No sweetness remains in your holy places.

Now I can speak to Rome as the prophet once spoke to Jerusalem—where people used to live in righteousness and where princes loved peace. But now Rome has turned the color of rust. Its princes are murderers. Romans, your days are numbered; you should be mourning rather than rejoicing.[15]

This prophetic and determined woman was right: the century after Celestine V was disastrous for the faithful, and the Church was in shambles. While Boniface VIII was still in power, Jacopone of Todi poignantly wrote:

Where are the Fathers, once filled with faith?
Where are the Prophets, full of hope and praise?
Where are the Apostles, filled with zeal?
Where are the Martyrs, full of strength?
Not one comes near.

All of these events—the popes' claims of power and spiritual authority, the fleeing of successive popes to Avignon, counter-popes and antipopes, the second great schism of Christianity, and eventually, what became the Reformation—fell hard on the heels of what happened in 1294–96. One wonders if Celestine could have reformed the Church and put it on a different course from the one it would follow. He saw the problems clearly enough, but his decision not to act sent the papacy and the Catholic Church in these unfortunate directions.

IS SAINT *ENOUGH*?

One Sunday morning when Peter Morrone was a young hermit, one of his spiritual brothers had a vision. An angel appeared to him and said, "Have you noticed in the oratory where all of you pray, how the lamp moves back and forth in the air without anyone touching it? This is a sign that God is with you." From that moment on, Peter's Autobiography says, all of the hermits in that place were witness to this wonder, and there remained no question about the divine presence in their midst.

Not long afterward, on a Sunday evening, as the hermits were about to rise in the middle of the night to pray vigils, the devil grabbed four of them in such a way, the Autobiography says, that they cried out for help. One of them lifted his hands to the sky in fear and all who saw him witnessed that his fingers were twisted and deformed. The holy men were scared out of their wits. Then Peter (who describes himself humbly as "the brother who was at that time still in his cell") heard what was happening and went to see it firsthand. Without hesitation Peter told the others, "Whoever is able, keep praying!" By that next morning, prayer had overcome the evil spirits and they were gone from that place.

This was the work of Peter Morrone's entire life: to keep praying despite whatever happened. In the century after Peter's death, Petrarch would defend Peter's decision to abdicate as evidence that he understood his most important calling of all—to be a contemplative:

> Renouncing the papacy was an awful burden, he
> anxiously returned to his previous way of solitude.
> It was as if he'd freed himself from the clutches of
> an enemy. One could attribute this to cowardice,
> but seeing what were his true gifts, I see it another
> way. I praise him for making himself once again
> most useful to the world.[1]

Petrarch praises Peter for leaving the Holy See behind in order to do what he did best. The essential work of a contemplative monk is to pray for the world—to offer up to God, with the utmost attention and persistence, what the rest of us do not bother to offer. It has always been a comfort to Christians to know that men such as Peter are praying for them, even when they do not or cannot pray for themselves.

Is this what we are to make of the life and legacy of Peter Morrone-cum-Celestine V?

There is a miniature painting, a manuscript illumination housed in the Vatican Libraries, depicting James Stefaneschi interviewing the retired Celestine. In the simple, arresting image, James the historian sits at a scribe's desk with pen in hand before a bearded and slightly confused-looking Celestine, who is peeking out of the small window of his hermitage of Onofrio. The sense is that no one will ever quite know the essence or heart of that essentially very private man.[2]

In Catholic history, this tale ends in heavenly glory. A Catholic believes that he or she will one day know the truth of all things in the life to come. Saints know this more quickly than others. Less than a decade after Peter's death, Pope Clement V instructed the archbishop of Naples to begin a formal inquiry into Peter's sanctity. More than three hundred witnesses appeared before the religious court that was assembled in 1307, representing all walks of late-medieval society, testifying to his character, his witness, and the miraculous nature of Peter's life.[3] The austerities of his life were testified to. Nineteen miracles were presented by witnesses who had prayed to Peter for help to cure their illnesses, and fourteen of these were confirmed as irrefutable evidence, or true miracles, since the diseases were otherwise known to be incurable.[4]

It is rare that a saint's reputation is fixed before a century has gone by since his death, and in Peter's case there were competing claims and visions about his martyrdom, resignation, piety, and incompetence. All of this played out during the hearings, and on May 5, 1313, Clement V declared that God had made Peter a saint. The pope preached a homily that day on a short text from the prophet Isaiah: "Shout, and sing for joy, O inhabitant of Zion, for great in your midst is the Holy One of Israel" (Is. 12:6). Peter Morrone was henceforward to be known as Saint Pope Celestine V and his relics would be permanently housed in the church in L'Aquila.

Alban Butler begins his entry for May 19, the traditional feast day for Saint Pope Celestine V, with this somewhat shocking statement: "In all papal history no figure is more pathetic than that of Peter di Morone."[5] How odd that seems by this time in our story. What happened to Peter was the stuff of pathos, but was he pathetic? It was Edward Gibbon who said, "The pathetic almost always consists in the detail of little events." It is true that many of the details of the last two years of Celestine's life were miserable, eliciting pity, but the full meaning of his life, his motivations and decisions, amounts to much more than that. Still, two and a half centuries would go by before the world would see another pope raised to the ranks of the saints (Pius V), and no pope has ever taken the name Celestine, since.

Peter's Autobiography ends when he was only about thirty years old. What does it mean that he left no record of his doings or feelings beyond that time? It is as if nothing very important happened in Peter's life once he found his way from the monastery to the mountains. Perhaps in the hermit's mind that was true. A fierce and independent character, he always valued remote locations as spiritual teachers more than wise elders. He loved his life as a religious man, and he embraced the austerities of eremitism with gusto. And yet he was no simple hermit. Peter had a conflicting relationship with power and position; he had shown an interest in both as a younger man, and then in later life a lack of understanding of both. Lacking a subtle mind, he didn't trouble himself or his followers with theological or spiritual controversies. This tendency worked in his favor while he was a hermit, but it worked against him in the papacy. While he served as pope, the cardinals and curia must have been both baffled and threatened by how Peter often opted for an evangelical purity that they viewed as too simple.

It is intriguing that a monk who valued humility and privacy would come to sit on the throne of Saint Peter at all—a throne that came with both the keys to heaven and a sword to hold over the heads of all the inhabitants on earth. As Frederick Rolfe once riffed about the character of late-medieval churchmen, "Now we pretend to be immaculate, then they bragged of being vile." But this angelic pope was cut from a different cloth. To illustrate the point, playwright Peter Barnes has Celestine innocently say to one of his cardinals, "What has Christ's Church to do with monies and taxes?"

"Everything, Your Holiness. Everything," the cardinal responds.[6]

A Saint of Paradoxes

The traditional way of understanding all of this is to say that Peter was a naïve saint: a man who couldn't function in a world of scheming and sin because of his otherworldly holiness. This sentiment is expressed again and again in the late-medieval chronicles and stories about him. If Shakespeare had written a tragedy about Celestine, naïveté would have been his fatal character flaw. If an opera were written about him, Celestine's character would sing dramatic arias about his devotion to God without noticing the powerful men scheming in the dark recesses on stage behind him. Eamon Duffy represents this common interpretation when he refers simply to "the saintly but hopeless monk-hermit Celestine V."[7]

King Solomon is supposed to have said, "Like a lame man's legs, which hang useless, is a proverb in the mouth of fools" (Prv. 26:7). In other words, just as the legs of a disabled man might be of no use to him, so is wisdom of no use to a fool. Peter was the Don Quixote sort of fool: one who either doesn't realize his buffoonery or acts the jester in order to make a deeper point. But which was it? He donned simple clothing. He rode an ass to his coronation. He insisted on eating almost nothing while pope—"munching a dry loaf . . . declaring it the only savory food"[8]—and acted simply. He behaved in ways that were unlike any pope before or after him. During his brief papal sojourn, he safeguarded the rights of the Spiritual Franciscans who were being physically threatened by leaders of their order and were, themselves, accused of being fools. He refused to fight, to play the political games that his contemporaries expected of him. As a scholar of the Franciscan movement has summarized it, "The reign of this holy but most inefficient of Popes was a short and unhappy one, and his successors were men of a very different stamp."[9] But was Peter *foolish*?

The hagiographers will say he didn't know any better—that's the sort of fool that Peter was. This "innocent as doves" explanation is one way of looking at his failures. Some historians put it most critically: "The fact was that, for all his piety and reputation for holiness, the new pope was hopelessly naïve, almost ridiculously incompetent, and rather ill educated—a dangerous combination in those troubled times."[10]

In the end, looking at the full breadth of his life, both of these interpretations miss the mark. There is more to the pope who quit than saintliness and foolish ineptitude. Peter had as much charisma as he possessed piety, and he was bold and perhaps arrogant enough to be a medieval pope. He'd been an able organizer and charismatic leader.

He clearly had the ability to stir souls by the power of his personal presence. His ascetic qualities were unflaggingly inspiring to those who were drawn to him, wanting also to renounce a confusing and dispirited worldly existence for the Kingdom of Heaven. By most accounts, "[Peter Morrone] had a remarkable record as the creator of a congregation of hermits within the Benedictine order."[11] Why then did this accomplished man become an incredibly incompetent pope? "His reign was an absurdity; under the thumb of Charles . . . a few months reduced the Curia to chaos," quips Edward Armstrong in *The Cambridge Medieval History*.[12]

I believe that the solution to this puzzle is not to be found in the theories of foolishness or holy naïveté. Instead, it is hinted at in this comment from contemporary British writer A. N. Wilson: "I bend my knee to the unwilling holy man who knew there was no meeting place between the pursuit of power and the worship of God."[13]

Peter clearly wasn't simple. He wasn't a mountaintop hermit without regard for public opinion. "Ignorant of the intricacies of papal business, too old and dreamy to shape a resolute policy, he longed for solitude," as one historian has put it.[14] But his story isn't that easy either. It's not that he was so adept at mystical spiritual practices that a taste for power and influence had been driven from him. That's not what comes through most clearly in the stories from those days.

Perhaps he found himself unable to function, psychologically and spiritually, in the midst of the power plays of the loggia and the court. He'd succeeded brilliantly in organizing and leading a monastic order of his own founding, in a situation where he was the only minister-general, but when forced to engage with others holding alternative views, he folded. He became spineless. Was he able to lead only when he would lead completely unchallenged?

Perhaps, but in all of the mess of those fifteen weeks, it is intriguing to consider an alternative possibility. Was Celestine essentially an obscurantist? Perhaps he wasn't inept so much as he was ruling from a stance of passive protest. Shocked to discover what it meant to be holy father, he may have quietly resolved at some point simply not to do it. Perhaps he believed himself to be the head of an ecclesiastical bureaucracy that he didn't acknowledge as entirely legitimate as it was structured. This theory would explain many of his actions in office and would also fit the pattern of where he had come from. But ultimately the evidence also points to something that Dante said long ago.

A Moral Failing

Perhaps it was once possible to be a heavenly saint without being a human one. To have spiritual qualities without using them to respond to the world one is confronted with. We wouldn't allow this contradiction to stand today. And not everyone did then either. For his moral failures, Dante assigned Peter to milling around the vestibule of the *Inferno* for eternity:

> *And after it there came so long a train*
> *Of people, that I ne'er would have believed*
> *That ever Death so many had undone.*

When some among them I had recognised,
I looked, and I beheld the shade of him
Who made through cowardice the great refusal.[15]

This "great refusal" (*gran rifiuto*) was Dante's way of expressing Peter's unforgiveable sin: cowardice. He didn't even have to name Peter in that passage since his readers knew what had happened. The abdication was fresh in their memories.

Still, there are other theories about why Dante didn't explicitly name Peter. Some believe he intended Pontius Pilate, who, rather than following his own conscience, showed cowardice by releasing Christ into the hands of those who would crucify him. Others have guessed that Dante meant Flavius Claudius Julianus Augustus, who became known as Julian the Apostate. In any case, none of these characters is great company. *The Dante Encyclopedia* probably puts it best when it suggests that not naming the object of his contempt was precisely Dante's intent—it was yet another way to emphasize what he believed to be Peter's complete lack of character.[16] No one likes a quitter. As one historian has pithily phrased it, this means that Peter's entire papacy was "an act of pusillanimous irresponsibility."[17]

Could It Happen Today?

The angelic pope responded to power in the only ways he knew how. He retreated and prayed. But that wasn't enough.

The *New York Times* ran a story in April 2010 that began this way: "He is elected for life, by a group of elderly men infused with the will of God. People address him as Holy Father, not Mr. President. After bishop of Rome, his second title is vicar of Jesus Christ. Can a man like this quit his job?" The occasion for the story was to reflect on the possibility that the current Pope Benedict XVI could possibly abdicate.[18] It's not likely that he ever will. Nevertheless, some of Benedict XVI's most recent predecessors were rumored to have considered stepping down.

Pope Paul VI is the only sitting pontiff ever to visit Celestine's Fumone castle; he did so on September 1, 1966, and delivered a speech in which he showed admiration for the angelic pope. The precise reasons for this visit were never fully explained, although at the same time the sixty-nine-year-old pope urged all priests to consider retiring when they turn seventy-five, for the sake of the Church. Some in the media speculated that Paul VI might have been considering an abdication himself.[19] Six years later his seventy-fifth birthday would come and go. Paul VI died in office in 1978.

Twenty years after the suggestion of Paul VI's considerations, the hints of Pope John Paul II's possible abdication began around the issue of his spending too little time focusing on administrative issues, leaving the running of the Vatican to others. Looking back, one observer has reflected: "While he lost nothing of his strength and power, the glory of his office, Wojtyla seemed at times almost sad about his own elevated position, suggesting that his real life was the one he spent alone in prayer and contemplation, the one we had seen when he sat without moving, his face covered. He was offering this rich private life of his to the

crowd as the life they could have if they followed him."[20]
This sounds almost precisely like the papacy of Celestine V. How intriguing it is to imagine our hermit in the
light of this most recent and famous of papal examples.
John Paul II's biographer characterizes what happened
during his papacy by saying, "[H]e was reinventing the
papacy as an office of evangelical witness rather than
bureaucratic management."[21]

There are many differences between the two papacies,
and the successes of John Paul II are surely much more
numerous than were the failures of Celestine V. However,
the most profound difference of all is that Celestine lived
and ruled long before the digital and television age. There
could be no positive effect of a profound personal, spiritual witness in a pope in 1294 that could compare to the
effect today, when millions of faithful are able to witness
images of piety in their holy father every day, live, stream-
ing on the Internet or broadcast on television. A pope had
no hope of saving the world through piety alone seven
hundred years ago.

Being too good and holy to put his energy into acquir-
ing the political savvy necessary to a medieval pontiff simply made Celestine appear inept. He was "pious but weak
and incapable," as one historian has written.[22]

Similar arguments have been recently made about
Pope Benedict XVI. Incidents such as the 2006 Regens-
burg University speech, when he referred to Islam as "evil
and inhuman," and in 2010 as he failed to manage another
growing sexual abuse scandal, have led some to say that a
lack of administrative and diplomatic skills—the same sort
of ineptitude shown by Celestine V—might be grounds for
a twenty-first-century pope to resign.

Could it happen today? On a Sunday in April 2010, a

parish priest in Massachusetts became the first authority from within the Catholic Church to suggest that this pope should quit. The story ran on the front page of *The Boston Globe,* with Reverend James J. Scahill of East Longmeadow, Massachusetts, telling about how he had received a standing ovation at Mass that day. "The right thing is to be truthful, and if he is not up to dealing with this, then he should have the integrity to resign," he said, summarizing his sermon from that day.[23]

Since that time it has become clear that Benedict XVI is willing to engage with the problems that the Church faces. He has never been, and will never be, a leader like Celestine V. Yet Benedict XVI has chosen to align his papacy with the memory of our hermit pope. As you may recall from earlier in this book, he laid his pallium on Celestine's tomb in April 2009. Also consider this incredible paragraph from Benedict's first homily at his Mass of inauguration exactly four years earlier:

> One of the basic characteristics of a shepherd must be to love the people entrusted to him, even as he loves Christ whom he serves. "Feed my sheep," says Christ to Peter, and now, at this moment, he says it to me as well. Feeding means loving, and loving also means being ready to suffer. Loving means giving the sheep what is truly good, the nourishment of God's truth, of God's word, the nourishment of his presence, which he gives us in the Blessed Sacrament. My dear friends—at this moment I can only say: pray for me, that I may learn to love the Lord more and more. Pray for me, that I may learn to

> love his flock more and more—in other words, you,
> the holy Church, each one of you and all of you
> together. Pray for me, that I may not flee for fear
> of the wolves.

It is impossible to read these words now—especially the last sentence—without recalling the life and death of Celestine V.

Italian historian Sergio Luzzatto has said, "Saints exist mainly to perform miracles."[24] And for those who pray to the saints, asking for help in some particular aspect of life, it's never been quite clear what Saint Pope Celestine V is good for. Alban Butler long ago said that Celestine should be the saint of retirees: "Those who are destined by heaven to a retired life, in it become most eminently serviceable to the world, by proving excellent examples of innocence, and the perfect spirit of every Christian virtue, and by their prayers and continual pure homages of praise and thanksgivings to God, from which others may reap far more valuable benefits than from the labors of the learned or the bountiful alms of the rich." The hermit pope has also been claimed as the patron saint of bookbinders, and of L'Aquila. None of these is very compelling.

Celestine V's original coronation took place on August 28, 1294, and to this day each year on August 28 the holy doors of the Basilica of Santa Maria of Collemaggio are ceremoniously opened and pilgrims flood inside. Despite the fact that one of Boniface VIII's first acts was to rescind what has come to be known as the Saint Celestine Pardon (the plenary indulgence he granted for those who come), the festivities are still broad and colorful. Celestine's original bull is read out to the public and then publicly displayed until midday the following day. It is an occasion for festive celebration as well as some traditional confession and reconciliation between the devout and their priests. On at least those two days, thousands of people consider who this man was.

There is clearly more to this saint than retirement, bookbinding, or a small town in Italy.

Finally, the story of Celestine V warns us of the dangers of religious power: giving us some insight into how to know when it is being inappropriately wielded, and what to do to appropriately diminish it. Ignazio Silone was the first person to suggest as much in the introduction to his book *The Story of a Humble Christian.* He recounts saying something to that effect to a simple Italian peasant whom he met along the path toward the Onofrio hermitage on Mount Morrone. And then, "When the peasant finally understood the meaning . . . he was overcome with irrepressible hilarity," Silone writes. "Afterwards, he said gravely: 'Then he's not a saint for us poor people; he's for the priests.' "[25] And perhaps that's the truest statement of all.

In the end, no life may be easily understood. Does the cowardice of Celestine's final years of life provide the best summary of who he was? I don't believe so.

Peter was a man of paradoxes rather than a cookie-cutter saint. When the entourage marched up Morrone to tell him of the papal election, perhaps the wisest instinct he'd ever had was the one that told him to flee. He *should* have run. It wasn't that he did not know, or was unprepared for, the rigors of the corrupt late-medieval papacy. He knew better.

His sanest expectations were confirmed within weeks of ascending the chair of St. Peter, prompting him to make the decision that would save his soul—if not the Church. He quit. And for that single act, he showed himself to be enlightened, not naïve.[26]

NOTES

TIME LINE OF KEY EVENTS

1. In the Middle Ages and until 1939, L'Aquila was known simply as *Aquila*, but for purposes of clarity, the town is referred to by its current name throughout this book.

PROLOGUE

1. Despite the fact that seventy-five years ago, Maurice Powicke wrote the following overstatement: "Few episodes in medieval history are better known than the brief pontificate of Pope Celestine V in the year 1294." Sir Maurice Powicke, *The Christian Life in the Middle Ages: And Other Essays* (New York: Oxford University Press, 1935), 50.
2. Dante, *Inferno,* canto III, lines 58–60. All quotations from Dante's *Divine Comedy* are taken from the legendary translation of Henry Wadsworth Longfellow.
3. Anne MacDonell, *Sons of Francis* (New York: G. P. Putnam's Sons, 1902), 318.
4. I am particularly indebted to *Medieval Italy: Texts in Translation,* ed. Katherine L. Jansen, Joanna Drell, and Frances Andrews (Philadelphia: University of Pennsylvania Press, 2009).

INTRODUCTION

1. Monsignor Slawomir Oder with Saverio Gaeta, *Why He Is a Saint: The Life and Faith of Pope John Paul II and the Case for Canonization* (New York: Rizzoli, 2010). Oder made this announcement in January 2010 when the book was first published in Italian. The English translation was published in October 2010.

2. These public assemblies were outlawed by papal decree of Pope Clement VI in 1349.

3. Luke 9:58. All quotations from the Holy Bible are taken from the Revised Standard Version, Second Catholic Edition.

4. Sophia Menache, *Clement V* (New York: Cambridge University Press, 1998), 202.

CHAPTER 1

1. See Emma Dench, *From Barbarians to New Men: Greek, Roman, and Modern Perceptions of Peoples of the Central Apennines* (New York: Clarendon Press, 1995), 127.

2. Dench, *From Barbarians to New Men,* 111.

3. Consider the handwritten note that a young King Henry VIII addressed in French to his lover Anne Boleyn, pledging loyalty to her despite the fact that he was already married to Catherine of Aragon. With that letter, some historians believe, Henry committed himself to the course of action that would end his marriage and lead to England's formal break with Rome and the Catholic Church. It is owned and housed today in the Vatican Museum.

4. Quoted in Raymond Clemens and Timothy Graham, *Introduction to Manuscript Studies* (Ithaca, NY: Cornell University Press, 2007), 6.

CHAPTER 2

1. Jonathan Riley-Smith, *The Crusades: A History, Second Edition* (New York: Continuum, 2005), 192–93.

2. Eleven years after the siege that brought down Acre, only one small island off the Syrian coast remained in Christian hands, and then it too was lost. Centuries would go by before Christians would again travel freely to or reside in the Holy Land. Napoleon attempted an unsuccessful attack on Acre in 1799.

3. Peter Barnes, *Sunsets and Glories* (London: Methuen Drama, 1990), 1.1.2.

4. Quoted in Patricia Ranft, *The Theology of Work: Peter Damian and the Medieval Religious Renewal Movement* (New York: Palgrave Macmillan, 2006), 50.

5. T. S. R. Boase, *Boniface VIII* (Toronto: Macmillan, 1933), 29.

6. Niccolò Machiavelli, *The Prince: A New Translation*, trans. Harvey C. Mansfield, Jr. (Chicago: University of Chicago Press, 1985), 46.

7. Saint Irenaeus of Lyons, Tertullian, and Hegesippus. See John-Peter Pham, *Heirs of the Fisherman: Behind the Scenes of Papal Death and Succession* (New York: Oxford University Press, 2004), 42.

8. Pham, *Heirs of the Fisherman*, 45–59.

9. See Frederick J. Baumgartner, *Behind Locked Doors: A History of the Papal Elections* (New York: Palgrave Macmillan, 2003), 39–41.

10. It wasn't until the Western Schism in 1378 that all papal elections would take place at what we now know as Vatican City. Only in the last century have they always taken place in the Sistine Chapel. Each elector of a conclave has to make a solemn oath that he will keep the secrets within those walls, and he makes a vow not to serve the interests of any nation or government other than the Church in his discernment and voting.

11. Giovanni Boccaccio describes such a scene—a similar summer of plague in Florence one generation later—in the introduction to his *Decameron,* colorfully painting the picture of what was probably happening during those summers of 1292–94: "Some say it descended on the human race through the influence of heavenly bodies. Others say it was a punishment of God's righteous anger looking on our iniquitous ways. . . . The plague began in the early spring in a terrifying manner. It didn't take the form it had assumed in the East, where if one began to bleed from the nose it was a sign of certain death. Here, its earliest symptom in men and women was the appearance of swellings in the groin or armpit, sometimes egg-shaped and other times the size of an apple. . . . Very few people ever recovered from it . . . and whenever those in suffering mixed with those who were unaffected, it rushed onward with the speed of fire spreading through dry wood or oil. . . . This led some people to callously say there was no way to remedy against a plague than to run from it—and without thinking of anyone but themselves, large numbers abandoned the city, their homes, relatives, and belongings, and headed for the countryside." (My own translation. Compare to Giovanni Boccaccio; *The Decameron,* trans. G. H. McWilliam [New York: Penguin Books, 1972], 50–53.)

CHAPTER 3

1. Frederick J. Baumgartner, *Behind Locked Doors: A History of the Papal Elections* (New York: Palgrave Macmillan, 2003), 44.
2. Edward Armstrong, in *The Cambridge Medieval History, Vol. 7, Decline of Empire and Papacy* (Cambridge, UK: Cambridge University Press, 1964), 4.
3. Sir Maurice Powicke, *The Christian Life in the Middle Ages: And Other Essays* (New York: Oxford University Press, 1935), 50.
4. It was Philip the Fair and the Colonnas who would, sixteen

years later, pressure Pope Clement V to canonize Celestine V, in part as a rebuke to the papacy of Boniface VIII.

5. This is my own rendering. A previous version in English can be found in G. G. Coulton, *Life in the Middle Ages* (New York: Macmillan, 1935), vol. 1, 235.

6. Quoted in Peter Hebblethwaite, *The Year of Three Popes* (New York: Collins, 1979), 56.

7. All quotations from John Paul II's "Apostolic Constitution," *Universi Dominici Gregis,* are taken from the English-language translation available on the Vatican's website. Composing a document such as this was not in itself suggestive of anything; many popes throughout history have sought to bring the rules of conclaves and elections into a contemporary perspective.

8. It wasn't until the end of the Great Schism (1378–1417), when two men simultaneously claimed to be pope, that elections were consistently held in Rome, and it wasn't until the sixteenth century that a strict conclave was consistently maintained during papal elections. Since the February 1878 election of Pope Leo XIII, every papal election has been decided by a two-thirds majority vote from within the safe, enclosed hall of the Sistine Chapel.

9. Instead of leaking anything, Cardinal John Joseph Carberry, archbishop of Saint Louis (USA), said at a press conference the day after the election of John Paul II: "I would like to tell you everything. It would thrill you. But I can't." Quoted in Hebblethwaite, *The Year of Three Popes,* 146.

CHAPTER 4

1. Norbert Ohler, *The Medieval Traveller,* trans. Caroline Hillier (Woodbridge, UK: Boydell Press, 1995), 66.

2. For example, see Peter Herde, "Celestine V," in Philippe Levillain, general editor, *The Papacy: An Encyclopedia,* vol. 1 (New York: Routledge, 2002), 279–83.

3. T. S. R. Boase, *Boniface VIII* (Toronto: Macmillan, 1933), 37–38.
4. "Donation of Constantine," *The Catholic Encyclopedia* (New York: Robert Appleton Company, 1913).

CHAPTER 5

1. William Langland from *Piers the Ploughman,* quoted in Virginia Davis, "The Rule of Saint Paul the First Hermit," in *Monks, Hermits and the Ascetic Tradition,* ed. W. J. Sheils (London: Basil Blackwell, 1985), 213.
2. Thomas Aquinas, in *Albert and Thomas: Selected Writings,* ed. Simon Tugwell (Mahwah, NJ: Paulist Press, 1988), 559. Aquinas was also a strong advocate for the need of the state to aid human beings to find full happiness. He wrote: "It is . . . necessary for man to live in a multitude so that each one may assist his fellows, and different men may be occupied in seeking, by their reason, to make different discoveries—one, for example, in medicine, one in this and another in that." (Quoted in Dino Bigongiari, *Essays on Dante and Medieval Culture* [New York: Griffin House, 2000], 106.)
3. *Peter Damian Letters 151–180,* trans. Owen J. Blum and Irven M. Resnick (Washington, DC: Catholic University of America Press, 2005), 181.
4. Sophia Menache, *Clement V* (New York: Cambridge University Press, 1998), 202.
5. T. S. R. Boase, *Boniface VIII* (Toronto: Macmillan, 1933), 42.
6. John-Peter Pham, *Heirs of the Fisherman: Behind the Scenes of Papal Death and Succession* (New York: Oxford University Press, 2004), 72.
7. Caroline Bruzelius, *The Stones of Naples: Church Building in Angevin Italy 1266–1343* (New Haven, CT: Yale University Press, 2004), 172.

CHAPTER 6

1. See Robert Brentano, "Sulmona Society and the Miracles of Peter of Morrone," *Monks and Nuns, Saints and Outcasts: Religion in Medieval Society (Essays in Honor of Lester K. Little)*, ed. Sharon Farmer and Barbara H. Rosenwein (Ithaca, NY: Cornell University Press, 2000).

2. Estella Canziani, *Through the Apennines and the Lands of the Abruzzi: Landscape and Peasant Life* (Cambridge, UK: W. Heffer and Sons, 1928), 183.

3. I have slightly paraphrased the quotations from the Autobiography of Celestine V. See *Other Middle Ages: Witnesses at the Margins of Medieval Society*, ed. Michael Goodich (Philadelphia: University of Pennsylvania Press, 1998), 170–80.

4. In our own day (since 1963) the two regions have been separated. As a result, today's Molise no longer includes the Morrone and Maiella mountains.

5. Canziani, *Through the Apennines and the Lands of the Abruzzi*, 5.

6. John Hooper, "Pope Visits Italian Village Hit Hardest by Earthquake," *Guardian*, London, April 28, 2009.

7. Ignazio Silone, *Fontamara*, trans. Harvey Fergusson II (New York: Atheneum, 1960), 3, 4, 5.

8. See Augustine Thompson, O.P., *Cities of God: The Religion of the Italian Communes 1125–1325* (University Park, PA: Penn State Press, 2005), 294–96.

9. John Shinners, ed., *Medieval Popular Religion 1000–1500: A Reader*, 2d ed. (Orchard Park, NY: Broadview Press, 2007), 19.

CHAPTER 7

1. Pope Nicholas III, *Exiit qui seminat*, trans. from the Latin and in the public domain: http.franciscan-archive.org.

2. John C. Moore, *Pope Innocent III (1160/61–1216): To Root*

Up and to Plant (Notre Dame, IN: University of Notre Dame Press, 2009), 11.

3. Umberto Pappalardo, *The Gulf of Naples: Archaeology and History of an Ancient Land,* trans. Peter Eustace (Verona, Italy: Arsenale Editrice, 2006), 126.

4. Otto, Bishop of Bamberg, in 1109. This translation is my own rendering. See G. G. Coulton, *Life in the Middle Ages,* vol. 4 (New York: Macmillan, 1935), 106–7.

CHAPTER 8

1. See Lisa M. Bitel, "Saints and Angry Neighbors: The Politics of Cursing in Irish Hagiography," in *Monks and Nuns, Saints and Outcasts: Religion in Medieval Society—Essays in Honor of Lester K. Little,* ed. Sharon Farmer and Barbara H. Rosenwein (Ithaca, NY: Cornell University Press, 2000), 123–50.

2. Letter 161 in *Peter Damian Letters 151–180,* trans. Owen J. Blum and Irven M. Resnick (Washington, DC: Catholic University of America Press, 2005), 133.

3. Letter 152 in *Damian Letters,* 7–9.

4. Letter 152 in *Damian Letters,* 9.

5. Saint Stephen's order was known as the Grandmontines and was mostly extinct by the late eighteenth century. See Brenda M. Bolton, "Via Ascetica: A Papal Quandary," in *Monks, Hermits and the Ascetic Tradition,* ed. W. J. Sheils (London: Basil Blackwell, 1985), 171–73.

6. Most sources do not identify the mountain of Peter's first years, but Peter Herde does in "Celestine V," in Philippe Levillain, general editor, *The Papacy: An Encyclopedia,* vol. 1 (New York: Routledge, 2002), 279–83.

7. The fifth-century Egyptian anchorite Abba Isaiah of Scetis wrote: "If you wish to ask an elder about some thought, bare your thought to him voluntarily, if you know that he is trustworthy and will keep your words." (*Abba Isaiah of Scetis: Ascetic Discourses,* trans. John Chryssavgis and Pachomios Penkett [Kalamazoo, MI: Cistercian Publications, 2002], 53.)

8. Both texts are taken from John T. McNeill and Helena M. Gamer, *Medieval Handbooks of Penance* (New York: Columbia University Press, 1938), 330–31. I have revised the translations slightly.

9. Anne MacDonell, *Sons of Francis* (New York: G. P. Putnam's Sons, 1902), 320.

10. This expression is from John Howe (quoting Ernst Werner), in "The Awesome Hermit: The Symbolic Significance of the Hermit as a Possible Research Perspective," *Numen* 30, no. 1 (July 1983): 106.

11. Also quoted by Howe in "The Awesome Hermit."

12. Today it's a national park, Parco Nazionale della Majella, with a website.

13. Ignazio Silone, *The Story of a Humble Christian*, trans. William Weaver (New York: Harper & Row, 1970), 17.

CHAPTER 9

1. Etienne Gilson, *The Mystical Theology of Saint Bernard*, trans. A. H. C. Downes (New York: Sheed & Ward, 1940), 18.

2. The image appeared in the pages of a history book written by Ludovico Zanotti. See Leonida Giardini et al., *Celestino V: e la sua Basilica* (Milan: Silvana Editoriale Spa, 2006), 52.

3. Peter Herde suggests that Joachim's influence is seen on Peter in the frequent inscriptions to the Holy Spirit that are found on monasteries he founded. See "Celestine V," in Philippe Levillain, general editor, *The Papacy: An Encyclopedia*, vol. 1 (New York: Routledge, 2002), 281. For more on this interpretation of history, see the discussion of Joachim of Fiore, in chapter 11.

4. Robert Brentano, "Sulmona Society and the Miracles of Peter of Morrone," in *Monks and Nuns, Saints and Outcasts: Religion in Medieval Society (Essays in Honor of Lester K. Little)*, ed. Sharon Farmer and Barbara H. Rosenwein (Ithaca, NY: Cornell University Press, 2000), x.

CHAPTER 10

1. See Pascal Montaubin, "Bastard Nepotism," in *Pope, Church, and City: Essays in Honour of Brenda M. Bolton*, ed. Frances Andrews et al. (Leiden, The Netherlands: Brill, 2004), 145–46.
2. Joseph F. Kelly, *The Ecumenical Councils of the Catholic Church: A History* (Collegeville, MN: Liturgical Press, 2009), 96.
3. George Lane, *Early Mongol Rule in Thirteenth-Century Iran: A Persian Renaissance* (New York: Routledge Curzon, 2003), 50.
4. Today, ironically, the hill of Collemaggio no longer exists because the valley attached to it was filled in during the nineteenth century by the local government in order to make pilgrimage to the Basilica of Santa Maria easier.
5. Peter Herde, "Celestine V," in Philippe Levillain, general editor, *The Papacy: An Encyclopedia*, vol. 1 (New York: Routledge, 2002), 280.

CHAPTER 11

1. This quotation is from the article on "Indulgences" from the old *Catholic Encyclopedia*, originally published in 1913, and currently available online at www.newadvent.org.
2. Jonathan Sumption, *Pilgrimage: An Image of Mediaeval Religion* (Totowa, NJ: Rowman & Littlefield, 1975), 142.
3. Quoted in Jonathan Riley-Smith, *The Crusades: A History*, 2d ed. (New Haven, CT: Yale University Press, 2005), 14.
4. The phrase "evangelical awakening" comes from Marie-Dominique Chenu, in *Nature, Man and Society in the Twelfth Century*, ed. J. Taylor and L. K. Little (Chicago: University of Chicago Press, 1968), ch. 7.
5. During the days of the Catholic Counter-Reformation, in 1571 a papal bull sought to suppress this loosely organized order after one of its members attempted to murder an emissary of Pope Pius V's, who'd been charged with reforming the group.

6. David Abulafia, ed., *Italy in the Central Middle Ages: 1000–1300* (New York: Oxford University Press, 2004), 11.

7. Peter Herde, "Literary Activities of the Imperial and Papal Chanceries during the Struggle between Frederick II and the Papacy," in *Intellectual Life at the Court of Frederick II Hohenstaufen,* ed. William Tronzo (Washington, DC: National Gallery of Art, 1994), 233.

8. Roger Bacon, quoted in Robert Bartlett, *The Natural and the Supernatural in the Middle Ages* (New York: Cambridge University Press, 2008), 125.

9. Roger Bacon, quoted in Bartlett, *The Natural and the Supernatural in the Middle Ages,* 129.

10. Marjorie Reeves, *The Influence of Prophecy in the Later Middle Ages: A Study in Joachimism* (Notre Dame, IN: University of Notre Dame Press, 1993), 5.

11. Bernard McGinn, *The Calabrian Abbot: Joachim of Fiore in the History of Western Thought* (New York: Macmillan, 1985), 153. All quotes from Joachim's writings are taken from this translation.

12. Marjorie Reeves, "Some Popular Prophecies from the Fourteenth to the Seventeenth Centuries," in *Popular Belief and Practice,* ed. G. J. Cuming and Derek Baker (New York: Cambridge University Press, 1972), 111.

CHAPTER 12

1. See Erik Thuno, *Image and Relic: Mediating the Sacred in Early Medieval Rome* (Rome: L'Erma di Bretschneider, 2002), 163–71. Thuno writes: "[T]he Lateran in the Middle Ages was often linked with the Old Testament temple . . . from the tenth century on to Mt. Sinai where the Law was given, and later . . . said to contain the actual Ark of the Covenant including its sacred contents within the high altar" (p. 165).

2. David Willey, "Agony of L'Aquila," *Tablet,* April 18, 2009, 8.

3. Susan Twyman, *Papal Ceremonial at Rome in the Twelfth Century* (London: Henry Bradshaw Society, 2002), 1–22.

4. T. S. R. Boase, *Boniface VIII* (Toronto: Macmillan, 1933), 40.

5. *Francis of Assisi: Early Documents, Vol. 1,* ed. Regis J. Armstrong et al. (Hyde Park, NY: New City Press, 1999), 86.

6. In 1279 Pope Nicholas III wrote a bull entitled *Exiit qui seminat,* trying to reconcile the two factions within the Franciscans. As a former protector of the order, he was in a privileged place to accomplish this. He succeeded to some extent, and his teachings showed a reasonable way forward—a possible, middle way. First, he affirmed Francis's teaching that Jesus and the disciples never owned a thing and never handled money—meaning that to truly imitate Christ, a Franciscan would do as Francis taught. But he then applied scholastic finery to the distinctions of what is to be defined as "money," what it means to have enough for the present and its needs, and how friars may have recourse to benefactors who have money. Many doors and windows were opened on the topic of the handling, obtaining, and use of money by friars after all.

7. *Angelo Clareno: A Chronicle or History of the Seven Tribulations of the Order of Brothers Minor,* trans. David Burr and Emmett Randolph Daniel (Saint Bonaventure, NY: Franciscan Institute Publications, 2005), 6–7.

8. See "Celestine V," *The Catholic Encyclopedia,* online at www.newadvent.org.

CHAPTER 13

1. Eamon Duffy, *Saints and Sinners: A History of the Popes,* 2d ed. (New Haven, CT: Yale University Press, 2001), xi.

2. Jean Dunbabin uses both descriptions for Charles I. See Jean Dunbabin, *Charles I of Anjou: Power, Kingship and State-Making in Thirteenth-Century Europe* (New York: Longman, 1998), 194, 198.

3. Richard Mortimer, *Angevin England: 1154–1258* (Cambridge, MA: Blackwell, 1994), 113.

4. Steven Runciman, *The Sicilian Vespers: A History of the Mediter-*

ranean World in the Later Thirteenth Century (New York: Cambridge University Press, 1958), 115.

5. T. S. R. Boase, *Boniface VIII* (Toronto: Macmillan, 1933), 46.

6. Lawrence V. Mott, *Sea Power in the Medieval Mediterranean: The Catalan-Aragonese Fleet in the War of the Sicilian Vespers* (Gainesville: University Press of Florida, 2003), 36.

7. It is from the Sicilian Vespers that we trace the origins of the geography of Sicily (the island only) that continues to today.

8. Caroline Bruzelius, *The Stones of Naples: Church Building in Angevin Italy 1266–1343* (New Haven, CT: Yale University Press, 2004), 242n75.

9. One contemporary Italian scholar, Roberto Paciocco, acknowledges their confusing relationship with the Church by writing that if one were to survey "the links between the Angevin dynasty and the Spirituals," the best conclusion "in all likelihood would be to describe the rulers' behavior as hovering between open support and conniving protection." Quoted in *The Church of Santa Maria Donna Regina: Art, Iconography and Patronage in Fourteenth-Century Naples*, ed. Janis Elliott and Cordelia Warr (Burlington, VT: Ashgate, 2004), 29.

10. As well as Alfonso III. However, Dante talks with Charles Martel in heaven in the *Paradiso*.

CHAPTER 14

1. John C. Moore, *Pope Innocent III (1160/61–1216): To Root Up and to Plant* (Notre Dame, IN: University of Notre Dame Press, 2009), 4.

2. Dino Bigongiari, *Essays on Dante and Medieval Culture* (New York: Griffin House, 2000), 23.

3. Quoted in David Abulafia, ed. *Italy in the Central Middle Ages: 1000–1300* (New York: Oxford University Press, 2004), 96.

4. The Lateran Treaty of 1929 would describe the creation of the Vatican State in these terms: "Italy recognizes the full ownership and the exclusive and absolute power and

jurisdiction of the Holy See over the Vatican as it is presently
constituted, together with all its appurtenances and endow-
ments, creating in this manner Vatican City for the special
purposes and under the conditions given in this Treaty. The
boundaries of the said City are set forth in the map which
constitutes Attachment I of the present Treaty, of which it
forms an integral part. It remains understood that St. Peter's Square, although forming part of Vatican City, will continue to be normally open to the public and to be subject
to the police power of the Italian authorities, who will stop
at the foot of the steps leading to the Basilica, although the
latter will continue to be used for public worship, and they
will, therefore, abstain from mounting the steps and entering the said Basilica, unless they are asked to intervene by
the competent authority. Whenever the Holy See considers it
necessary, for the purpose of particular functions, to close St.
Peter's Square temporarily to the free passage of the public,
the Italian authorities will withdraw beyond the outer lines
of Bernini's Colonnade and their extension, unless they have
been asked to remain by the competent authority." The complete text of the Lateran Treaty is available on a Vatican website: www.vaticanstate.va.

5. Jonathan Sumption, *Pilgrimage: An Image of Mediaeval Religion*
(Totowa, NJ: Rowman & Littlefield, 1975), 143.

6. See John Shinners, ed., *Medieval Popular Religion 1000–
1500: A Reader,* 2d ed. (Orchard Park, NY: Broadview Press,
2007), 404–5.

7. Eamon Duffy, *Saints and Sinners: A History of the Popes,* 2d ed.
(New Haven, CT: Yale University Press, 2001), 159.

8. Cardinal Gaetani, quoted in T. S. R. Boase, *Boniface VIII*
(Toronto: Macmillan, 1933), 48.

9. Castle Nuovo would remain at the center of political, com-
mercial, and artistic life in Naples for centuries. It was here,
thirty-five years later, that Giotto would spend a few years
painting. In 1347 the castle was sacked by King Louis I of
Hungary. The room known as Baron's Hall was made famous

in 1485 by a conspiracy hatched there against King Ferdinand I. The barons who conspired against the king were invited for a great feast, only for the doors to be shut upon them, and all of them arrested.

10. T. S. R. Boase, *Boniface VIII* (Toronto: Macmillan, 1933), 48.

11. Sophia Menache, *Clement V* (New York: Cambridge University Press, 1998), 23.

12. William Shakespeare, *Hamlet* 3.1.131–33.

13. Peter Herde, "Celestine V," in Philippe Levillain, general editor, *The Papacy: An Encyclopedia,* vol. 1 (New York: Routledge, 2002), 281.

14. James Brundage, *The Medieval Origins of the Legal Profession: Canonists, Civilians, and Courts* (Chicago: University of Chicago Press, 2010), 3–4.

15. Stefaneschi is quoted in E. R. Chamberlin, *The Bad Popes* (New York: Dial Press, 1969), 83.

16. John L. Allen, Jr. *Conclave: The Politics, Personalities, and Process of the Next Papal Election* (New York: Image Doubleday, 2002), 71.

CHAPTER 15

1. *St. Gregory the Great: Dialogues,* trans. Odo John Zimmerman (Washington, DC: Catholic University of America Press, 2002), 3–4.

2. John C. Moore, *Pope Innocent III (1160/61–1216): To Root Up and to Plant* (Notre Dame, IN: University of Notre Dame Press, 2009), 1.

3. Perhaps the most infamous case of warrior religious in Italy happened at the battle of Tusculum in the Marches of Ancona in 1167. The archbishops of Mainz and Cologne combined forces against a Roman army of 30,000 men and roundly defeated them. One contemporary chronicler reports, "In the morning the Romans hastened out to the battlefield to recover the corpses of their fallen. They were driven to flight by the bishops, who sent their knights out

against them. . . . Finally, they sent emissaries to the bishops to beg that they be allowed, for the love of Saint Peter and respect for Christianity, to recover their dead. The bishops granted this plea on the condition that they would count the number of men on their side that were killed or captured in this battle and would report this to them personally in writing with a sworn guarantee of their truthfulness. . . . When they went about this accounting, they found the number of some 15,000 of their men who had been killed or captured in this battle. After receiving permission, they buried the remains of their dead, which they recovered with loud lamenting." (See De Re Militari: The Society for Medieval Military History at http://www.deremilitari.orgRESOURCES/SOURCES/tusculum.htm.)

4. Frank Barlow, *Thomas Becket* (Sacramento: University of California Press, 1990), 68–69.

5. Dante, *Paradiso,* canto 9, lines 133–35.

6. T. S. R. Boase, *Boniface VIII* (Toronto: Macmillan, 1933), 49.

7. Quoted in Boase, *Boniface VIII,* 45.

8. This is from the testimony of James Stefaneschi, in book 3 of his *Opus Metricum.* The Orsini family had recently produced a pope in Nicholas III (1277–80), and Matthew Orsini would himself be elected pope on the first ballot on the first day of the conclave that was called after Celestine V resigned. He refused the job, and Cardinal Benedict Gaetani was then elected on the third day.

CHAPTER 16

1. *Peter Damian Letters 151–180,* trans. Owen J. Blum and Irven M. Resnick (Washington, DC: Catholic University of America Press, 2005), letter 165, p. 170–71.

2. *Peter Damian Letters,* letter 165, p. 173.

3. Adrian I, from *A Select Library of Nicene and Post-Nicene Fathers of the Christian Church,* vol. 14, *The Seven Ecumenical Councils* (Ann Arbor: University of Michigan Press, 1980), 536–37.

4. Quoted in various media, including the *Telegraph* (London), February 8, 2005.

5. In fact, this is the short statement that exists today in the Code of Canon Law of the Roman Catholic Church about the possibility of papal resignation: "If it happens that the Roman Pontiff resigns his office, it is required for validity that the resignation is made freely and properly manifested but not that it is accepted by anyone" (332 §2). The complete Canons are available on the Vatican's website: http://www.vatican.va/archive/ENG1104/__P16.HTM.

6. John of Paris, from the treatise *De potestate regia et papale*, quoted in Edward Peters, *The Shadow King: Rex Inutilis in Medieval Law and Literature 751–1327* (New Haven, CT: Yale University Press, 1970), 227–28.

CHAPTER 17

1. This is my rendering. The original Latin text appears in the classic, *Annales Ecclesiastici,* compiled by Odoricus Rainaldi, for the year 1294, number 20.

2. T. S. R. Boase, *Boniface VIII* (Toronto: Macmillan, 1933), 55.

3. John Eastman, "Holy Man of the Abruzzi and the Limitations of Papal Power," *Catholic Historical Review* 91, no. 4: 763.

4. Peter Barnes, *Sunsets and Glories* (London: Methuen Drama, 1990), 2.7.66.

CHAPTER 18

1. G. Geltner, *The Medieval Prison: A Social History* (Princeton, NJ: Princeton University Press, 2008), 86–87.

2. T. S. R. Boase, *Boniface VIII* (Toronto: Macmillan, 1933), 14–15.

3. Castle Fumone would haunt Boniface VIII long after the death of Peter Morrone. It was from Ferentino that William of Nogaret and fellow conspirators set out on September 6, 1303, to attack Boniface in Anagni on the following

day. They held and abused him for two days before escaping with their lives, leaving the pope to return to the relative safety of Rome.

4. This is suggested by David Burr in *Catholic Historical Review* 70 (April 1984): 297–98.

5. Eamon Duffy, *Saints and Sinners: A History of the Popes,* 2d ed. (New Haven, CT: Yale University Press, 2001), 104.

6. Duffy, *Saints and Sinners,* 104.

7. John Cornwell, *A Thief in the Night: The Mysterious Death of Pope John Paul I* (New York: Simon & Schuster, 1989), 47.

8. Peter Hebblethwaite, *The Year of Three Popes* (New York: Collins, 1979), 139. See also chapter 9, "The Thirty-three Day Pope," pp. 114–29.

9. For conspiracy theories see David Yallop's bestseller, *In God's Name: An Investigation into the Murder of Pope John Paul I* (New York: Basic Books, 2007). For a scholar's perspective see John Cornwell's *A Thief in the Night.*

10. Rainer Decker, *Witchcraft and the Papacy: An Account Drawing on the Formerly Secret Records of the Roman Inquisition,* trans. H. C. Erik Midelfort (Charlottesville: University of Virginia Press, 2008), 28. Pope Leo X (1513–21) was also plotted against—in this case by some of his cardinals. They attempted to poison him while treating him for an illness, but they were unsuccessful.

11. Biondo Flavio, *Italy Illuminated,* vol. 1, ed. and trans. Jeffrey A. White (Cambridge, MA: Harvard University Press, 2005), 161.

12. As reported by the Associated Press, "Monk Contends 13th-Century Pope Was Murdered with Nail," on August 20, 1998. As of March 1, 2011, large portions of Padre Quirino's work were available in English translation on his website: www.padrequirino.org/INTRO.PDF.

13. T. S. R. Boase, *Boniface VIII,* 369.

14. Much of the following discussion of poisons has been aided by Martin Levy's classic article, "Medieval Arabic Toxicology: The Book on Poisons of ibn Wahshiya and Its Relation to

Early Indian and Greek Texts," *Journal of the American Philosophical Society* 56, part 7 (1966): 5–130.

15. "Many positively asserted that by Nero's order his throat was smeared with some poisonous drug under the pretence of the application of a remedy, and that Burrus [the victim], who saw through the crime, when the emperor paid him a visit, recoiled with horror from his gaze, and merely replied to his question, 'I indeed am well.'" (*Complete Works of Tacitus,* trans. Alfred John Church and William Jackson Brodribb, ed. Moses Hadas [New York: Modern Library, 1942], 347.)

16. Levy, "Medieval Arabic Toxicology," 15.

17. Quoted in Brian Tierney, ed., *The Crisis of Church and State 1050–1300* (Englewood Cliffs, NJ: Prentice-Hall, 1964), 176–77.

18. T. S. R. Boase, *Boniface VIII,* 171.

19. Edward Peters, *The Shadow King: Rex Inutilis in Medieval Law and Literature 751–1327* (New Haven, CT: Yale University Press, 1970), 226.

20. Ernst H. Kantorowicz, *The King's Two Bodies: A Study in Medieaval Political Theology* (Princeton, NJ: Princeton University Press, 1997), 215n61.

21. Quoted in Charles T. Wood, ed., *Philip the Fair and Boniface VIII: State vs. Papacy,* 2d ed. (New York: Holt, Rinehart and Winston, 1971), 65.

CHAPTER 19

1. Émile Durkheim, *The Elementary Forms of the Religious Life* (New York: HarperCollins, 1976), 412.

2. *Angelo Clareno: A Chronicle or History of the Seven Tribulations of the Order of Brothers Minor,* trans. David Burr and Emmett Randolph Daniel (Saint Bonaventure, NY: Franciscan Institute Publications, 2005), 157.

3. Jacopone of Todi, *Laude* 35.

4. After Celestine V came Boniface VIII, and then Clement V in 1305. Like Celestine, Clement was lenient with the Spirituals

and pleaded with them to find monasteries in which to reside, wanting to bring a peaceful end to the controversies surrounding observance. As a result, three Franciscan monasteries saw an influx of Spirituals return, all in the Languedoc region of France. But within a few years, when both Clement and a sympathetic Franciscan minister-general (Alexander of Alexandria) had died, Conventual superiors were again appointed at these convents, and the conflict really heated up. The Spirituals were booted from the three monasteries, and they responded by attempting to take two of them by force. This won them quick, fresh excommunications, but the Spirituals persisted, this time by peaceful means, taking their appeal to yet another general chapter meeting of the order, in Naples in 1316. In the year following, Pope John XXII, at the urging of minister-general Michael of Cesena, brought a number of the Spirituals' leaders, including Angelo Clareno and Ubertino of Casale, to appear before him in Avignon for a doctrinal trial. They were ordered to submit to authority or be excommunicated and burned at the stake. "Great is poverty, but greater is obedience," Pope John infamously said. Twenty-five of these Spirituals were given over to an inquisitor, who, according to the euphemistic language of the *Catholic Encyclopedia*, "succeeded in converting twenty-one of them," which means they were tortured. The remaining four refused to acknowledge a religious authority higher than the original Rule of Saint Francis. These four were burned at the stake in Marseilles on May 7, 1318. The two most prominent Spirituals were spared: Ubertino of Casale, because he was defended in Avignon before the papal court by a sympathetic cardinal; and Angelo Clareno, because he fled for his life.

5. William J. Irons, trans., *Hymns Ancient and Modern, Standard Edition* (London: William Clowes and Sons, 1922), 459.

6. Jacopone of Todi, *Laude* 25.

7. *Defenders and Critics of Franciscan Life: Essays in Honor of John V.*

Fleming, ed. Michael F. Cusato and G. Geltner (Boston: Brill, 2009), 134.

8. Bernard Guenee, *Between Church and State: The Lives of Four French Prelates in the Middle Ages,* trans. Arthur Goldhammer (Chicago: University of Chicago Press, 1990), 216.

9. Paul Johnson, *The Renaissance: A Short History* (New York: Modern Library, 2000), 3.

10. Boniface VIII, *Unam Sanctam,* trans. Brian Tierney in *The Crisis of Church and State 1050–1300* (Englewood Cliffs, NJ: Prentice-Hall, 1964), 188.

11. Boniface, *Unam Sanctam.*

12. This translation is my own. For another, see *Bernard of Clairvaux: Five Books on Consideration—Advice to a Pope,* trans. John D. Anderson and Elizabeth T. Kennan (Kalamazoo, MI: Cistercian Publications, 1976), book 4, p. 3.

13. *Selected Letters of Pope Innocent III concerning England (1198-1216),* trans. C. R. Cheney and ed. C. R. Cheney and W. H. Semple (London: Thomas Nelson and Sons, 1953), 177, no. 67.

14. *Selected Letters of Pope Innocent III,* 188–89.

15. All extracts are from Saint Bridget of Sweden, *Liber Celestis,* book 3, ch. 27; the translations are mine.

CHAPTER 20

1. Francesco Petrarch, *De vita solitaria,* 2, 8.

2. Leonida Giardini et al., *Celestino V: e la sua Basilica* (Milan: Silvana Editoriale Spa, 2006), 56.

3. Michael Goodich, "The Politics of Canonization in the Thirteenth Century: Lay and Mendicant Saints," in *Saints and Their Cults: Studies in Religious Sociology, Folklore and History,* ed. Stephen Wilson (New York: Cambridge University Press, 1985), 181.

4. Sophia Menache, *Clement V* (New York: Cambridge University Press, 1998), 203.

5. Herbert J. Thurston and Donald Attwater, eds., *Butler's Lives*

of the Saints: Complete Edition, vol. 2 (London: Burns & Oates, 1956), 345.

6. Peter Barnes, *Sunsets and Glories* (London: Methuen Drama, 1990), 1.7.24.

7. Eamon Duffy, *Saints and Sinners: A History of the Popes,* 2d ed. (New Haven, CT: Yale University Press, 2001), 159.

8. T. S. R. Boase, *Boniface VIII* (Toronto: Macmillan, 1933), 45.

9. John R. H. Moorman, *The Sources for the Life of S. Francis of Assisi* (Manchester: Manchester University Press, 1940), 155.

10. John-Peter Pham, *Heirs of the Fisherman: Behind the Scenes of Papal Death and Succession* (New York: Oxford University Press, 2004), 72.

11. G. A. Holmes, review of the German edition of Peter Herde's biography of Celestine V, *English Historical Review* 97 (1982): 839.

12. Edward Armstrong, *The Cambridge Medieval History,* vol. 7, *Decline of Empire and Papacy* (Cambridge, UK: Cambridge University Press, 1964), 4.

13. A. N. Wilson, "Best Pope: The Pontiff Who Quit," *New York Times,* April 18, 1999.

14. Sir Maurice Powicke, *The Christian Life in the Middle Ages: And Other Essays* (New York: Oxford University Press, 1935), 51.

15. Dante, *Inferno,* canto 3, lines 55–60.

16. Peter Herde, "Celestine V, Pope," in *The Dante Encyclopedia,* ed. Richard Lansing (New York: Routledge, 2010), 152.

17. Herde, "Celestine V, Pope."

18. Daniel J. Wakin, "Do Popes Quit?" *New York Times,* April 10, 2010.

19. The speech is available on the Vatican website, but only in Italian: http://www.vatican.va/holy_father/paul_vi/speeches/1966/documents/hf_p-vi_spe_19660901_s-celestino-v_it.html. One example of the media speculation regarding Paul VI may be seen in this story from *Time,* September, 30, 1966: http://www.time.com/time/magazine/article/0,9171,836464,00.html.

20. Colm Toibin, "Among the Flutterers," *London Review of Books* 32, no. 16, August 19, 2010, 3–9.

21. George Weigel, *The End and the Beginning: Pope John Paul II—The Victory of Freedom, the Last Years, the Legacy* (New York: Doubleday, 2010), 2.

22. A. C. Flick, quoted in Charles T. Wood, ed., *Philip the Fair and Boniface VIII: State vs. Papacy*, 2d ed. (New York: Holt, Rinehart and Winston, 1971), 11.

23. Lisa Wangsness and Matt Rocheleau, "Amid Furor, Priest Gets Support," *Boston Globe*, April 13, 2010, A1.

24. Sergio Luzzatto, *Padre Pio: Miracles and Politics in a Secular Age*, trans. Frederika Randall (New York: Metropolitan Books, 2010), 4.

25. Ignazio Silone, *The Story of a Humble Christian*, trans. William Weaver (New York: Harper & Row, 1970), 18.

26. One recalls the prophetic words of Albino Luciani, the future Pope Paul I, on August 26, 1978, to the cardinals who elected him: "May God forgive you for what you have done to me." (Quoted in David Gibson's *The Rule of Benedict: Pope Benedict XVI and His Battle with the Modern World* [New York: HarperOne, 2007], 225.)

ACKNOWLEDGMENTS

I have many people to thank. My agent and friend, Greg Daniel, continues to be a sensitive ear and eye for all of my work, and for that I am grateful. My editor at Image Books, Gary Jansen, offered excellent vision and helpful coaching along the way. My wife, Michal, inspires me.

Many thanks, as well, to my friend and fellow traveler Brendan Walsh, who joined me in May 2009 to visit several locations in Assisi, Rome, and Naples relevant to this story. Thank you to the good people of Dartmouth College libraries in Hanover, New Hampshire, who so willingly and ably make their time and resources available to our local community.

This book has been the work, off and on, of the last three years, but most of it has been written in what Pope Benedict XVI declared to be the year of Saint Celestine, marking the eight-hundredth anniversary of Peter Morrone's birth in 1209. Thank you to the many friends who have endured breakfast and dinner conversations about Celestine V over the last year. Perhaps you wondered if the book would ever be finished and I would ever stop talking about "the pope who quit." From Steve Swayne many mornings at Lou's to Christina Brannock-Wanter at Stella's to Marjorie and Molly in Montpelier on Rosh Hashanah, thank you all for your indulgence, advice, and encouragement.

A note about some of the sources that are frequently quoted throughout the book: The selections from the *Laude* of the Franciscan friar Jacopone of Todi are my own renderings. The first translations of these verses into English were done by Jessie Beck and published in Evelyn Underhill's classic, *Jacopone of Todi: Poet and Mystic* (London and Toronto: J. M. Dent & Sons, 1919). Other translations are my own, as well, including those from Petrarch's "On the Solitary Life," and those from Boccaccio's *Decameron*. The endnotes indicate which translations are mine, and where to go to compare mine to others. The English quotations from Dante's *Divine Comedy* all come from the legendary translation of Henry Wadsworth Longfellow. Quotations from the Holy Scriptures are taken from the translation of the Revised Standard Version, Second Catholic Edition, used with permission.

INDEX